AF267432

HOW TO GO FROM BULLIED TO BOLD

By Teresa Robinson

Follow Teresa Robinson

Facebook: Teresa Rita Robinson
Instagram: @teresaritarobinson101768
LinkedIn: Teresa Rita Robinson
TikTok: teresaritarobinson
Website: bulliedtobold.com

CONTENTS

Dedication i

Acknowledgments iii

Introduction v

About the Author vii

Chapter 1: Bloodline 1

Chapter 2: Through The Eyes Behind The Glasses 15

Chapter 3: From The Porch To Purpose: Building Independence
After Life Changed 25

Chapter 4: The Pain I Carried, The Strength I Became 37

Chapter 5: Rising Through The Fire: A Mother's Strength,
A Worker's Journey 55

Chapter 6: Finding My Voice In Africa 61

Chapter 7: From Quiet Steps To Bold Stages 69

Chapter 8: From Bullied To Bold 89

Chapter 9: A Bold Legacy 95

Epilogue 103

From Bullied To Bold — A New Beginning 103

Dedication

This book is dedicated to the survivors: the ones who have walked through storms that seemed unbearable, the ones who cried in silence, the ones who wore smiles to cover pain, the ones who thought they were forgotten. You are not forgotten. You are not invisible. Your story matters.

It is also dedicated to every child who has ever been bullied, teased, or mocked for something they could not change. I see you. I was you. This book was written so that you will never again believe the lies others tell you about yourself.

To my son, Craig, you are my greatest inspiration. From the moment you were born, you gave me a reason to fight, even on the days when I wanted to give up. You are my reminder that love can break cycles, that hope can be passed down, and that resilience is inherited as much as it is taught. Everything I do, I do with you in mind.

To my parents, Edna and Albert Robinson, though you are gone, your love and your lessons live on inside of me. Mom, your quiet strength still whispers in my heart. Dad, your resilience in the face of hardship is etched into my spirit. I know that as I write these words and share this story with the world, you are both looking down with pride, smiling, and saying, "That's my girl."

To my siblings, both the ones who stood by me and the ones who turned away, you all shaped me. You forced me to choose boldness over bitterness, to rise above what was meant to hold me down.

To Shaun, thank you for saving me in ways I didn't know I needed saving. Thank you for showing me what it means to be loved without pain, for reminding me to love myself first, and for proving that respect and peace are not too much to ask for.

And finally, this book is dedicated to every reader who has picked it up in search of healing. I pray these words will remind you that no matter what you've endured, you are still here. You are stronger than you realize, and you can build a life filled with boldness, love, and purpose.

Acknowledgments

Gratitude is not just a word for me; it is a posture of my heart. Writing this book and reliving these memories was not easy, but I did not walk this journey alone.

To my son, Craig, you were my reason to endure. Your resilience, laughter, and determination carried me through my darkest days. You are my greatest accomplishment.

To my parents, Edna and Albert Robinson, thank you for the roots you gave me. Though I lost you too soon, your strength, love, and work ethic live on through me.

To my siblings, friends, and extended family, thank you for the memories, support, and reminders that I was never truly alone.

To my dear friend Dr. Denise Nicholson, your courage helped awaken my own voice.

To my Bold Tribe, thank you for showing me that boldness is a shared journey.

To Shaun, thank you for showing me what healthy love looks like and reminding me that I am enough.

And to every survivor and listener, this book is for you.

Above all, I thank God, who carried me through it all and turned my pain into purpose.

Introduction

Have you ever felt invisible? Have you ever looked in the mirror and hated what you saw staring back? Have you ever been laughed at until you cried, or carried bruises on your body that you lied about to protect someone else?

I have.

I grew up as the punchline before I had a chance to introduce myself. My thick glasses made me a target. My dark skin made me a joke. My pain made me a prisoner. I was bullied in classrooms, bruised in relationships, and overlooked at work. I learned how to smile when I was breaking, and to say "I'm fine" when I was anything but.

But this is not just a book about my pain. This is a book about my transformation.

Because somewhere along the way, I discovered that pain has a purpose. I discovered that silence can be broken. I discovered that affirmations are not just words, but lifelines. I discovered that therapy is not weakness, but strength. I discovered that faith does not prevent storms, but it anchors you through them. I discovered that I was not walking alone.

There were people God placed in my life who reminded me that even when I felt forgotten, I was not invisible: my son Craig, who gave me a reason to fight, my parents, who may be gone but whose love continues to echo in my heart. I know they are looking down, smiling, and saying, "That's our girl."

There were also friends who became family; people who listened when I finally dared to tell the truth, who held my hand through the tears and pushed me to keep speaking.

Then there was my dear friend, Dr. Denise Nicholson. Long before I stood on my own stage, I stood behind her, cheering her on as she boldly shared her story. Watching her taught me that authenticity is power. She reminded me that fear may shake your voice, but it cannot silence your purpose unless you let it. Denise helped me realize that my own voice was not just meant to stay in the shadows, it was meant to rise.

I also found strength in my Bold Tribe. They reminded me that boldness is not a solo act, it is a movement. They celebrated me when I doubted myself, lifted me when I stumbled, and surrounded me with the truth that we are stronger together. Their voices became a chorus of encouragement; a reminder that when one of us rises, we all rise.

This book is not just for children who are being laughed at in school. It is not just for women hiding bruises. It is not just for men who feel unseen. It is for anyone who has ever questioned their worth.

My hope is that these pages will meet you where you are but not leave you there; that you will see yourself in my story and find courage to write a new ending for yourself.

This is not just my testimony. It is an invitation to go from bullied to bold.

About the Author

Teresa Leola Robinson, also known as Rita, is a survivor, speaker, and author who transformed years of bullying, abuse, and loss into a powerful message of healing and boldness.

Born and raised in Mount Vernon, New York, Teresa grew up in a large and often complicated household where love and hardship existed side by side. She was the only Robinson sibling to graduate high school, and obtain a degree in business; a milestone she achieved despite relentless bullying, and the devastating loss of her mother at just fifteen. That moment defined her, not as a victim, but as a fighter who would keep moving forward no matter the obstacles.

Teresa went on to raise her son, Craig, largely on her own. He became her anchor, her greatest reason to push through pain, and the living proof that boldness can be inherited. She worked tirelessly, beginning her career in 1987 as a civilian employee with the Town of Greenburgh Police Department, where she has served for over 38 years. She later earned her college degree, balancing full-time work and single motherhood, proving that perseverance is stronger than circumstance.

In addition to her career, Teresa devoted over a decade to working with adults with autism, offering compassion and dignity to those who needed it most.

Her life has been filled with heartbreak, abusive relationships, betrayal, family loss, and the sting of being underestimated. Yet each challenge became fuel for her transformation. She found healing through therapy, the daily practice of affirmation, faith, and the love of people who reminded her of her worth.

In May 2025, Teresa stood on the TEDx stage in Clarkstown, New York, and shared her story with the world. That talk opened doors to international speaking engagements, including at the University of the West Indies in Jamaica, local opportunities to inspire youth in her community through the Greenburgh Police Department's Summer Youth Program, and a September 2025 engagement speaking with parents from G.O.O.D for girls (mentoring young girls into positive women). On September 24, 2025, she had the opportunity to speak on a panel for authors at The 54th Annual Legislative Conference (ALC), in Washington DC, October speaking to local schools and on October 11, 2025, she was the guest speaker via zoom for the Renew Your Mind Success Summit 2.0.

Teresa's journey has never been hers alone. She credits her dear friend Dr. Denise Nicholson, whose boldness on stage helped ignite her own courage to share her truth. She also acknowledges her Bold Tribe, a circle of encouragement and accountability that reminded her she was never walking alone. Together, they showed her that boldness is not just personal, it is communal, a movement that grows when voices rise together.

She is also deeply grateful to her partner, Shaun, who entered her life and showed her a new way of being loved, with patience, kindness, and respect. Through him, she learned that true love begins with loving herself first.

Today, Teresa is more than a survivor. She has a bold voice for healing, resilience, and change. Through her book, "How to Go From Bullied to Bold", she invites readers to rise above their pain, embrace their truth, and step boldly into the lives they were created to live.

CHAPTER 1

BLOODLINE

Affirmation: I am breaking generational patterns and choosing peace over pain.

Family was everything to us, not just a word, but a world. A universe unto itself, complete with its own gravity, its own rules, its own language of survival.

Growing up in the Taylor household meant living in a place where noise and laughter competed with arguments and tears, where love and pain often sat at the same table, passing dishes back and forth like they belonged together. Even at night, the house never truly slept. There was always movement: a baby crying somewhere in the maze of bedrooms, a sibling sneaking into the kitchen for leftover cornbread, my father's voice echoing through thin walls after he'd had too much to drink.

Our house was alive, sometimes too alive.

The floors creaked beneath the weight of too many footsteps: children running, adults shuffling, lives colliding in hallways too narrow to hold all our stories. Pots clanged in the kitchen as my mother called out, "Crystal!

Go to the store and get me some sugar!" Her voice cut through the chaos like a knife through butter.

The smell of food and family lingered in the air, sometimes comforting like Sunday morning biscuits, sometimes overwhelming like the grease that clung to everything after fish-fry Fridays. The walls held secrets; whispered arguments, muffled tears, belly laughs that shook the crooked pictures hanging on faded wallpaper.

We didn't have much money, but we had each other. While that sounds simple, even beautiful, it wasn't always easy. Having each other meant sharing clothes until the seams wore thin, arguing over the last biscuit at breakfast, and piling into cars for long summer trips down South, where the heat pressed against your skin and mosquitoes sang in your ears all night long.

It meant love: messy, complicated, sometimes painful love, and the kind of chaos that teaches you how to navigate storms before you ever learn what calm feels like.

I rarely heard my birth name at home. To my family, I was Crystal; a name that wrapped around me like a worn blanket, softened by years of use. It was how I was known, how I was loved, how I belonged to something bigger than myself.

"Jennifer" was for teachers who called roll without looking up. "Jennifer" was for bosses who didn't know me well enough to call me anything else. Jennifer felt formal, distant, official.

But Crystal? Crystal was for home. Crystal meant I belonged.

Not all names carried warmth.

At school, the nickname "Grandma Dynamite," given because of my thick glasses, stung deeply. Children don't realize how words can cut. They don't know that some wounds echo for years, that what they forget by recess can follow you home, climb into bed with you, and whisper itself into your dreams.

Yet at home, Crystal reminded me that I belonged to something bigger than my pain. Even when family felt like too much; too loud, too close, too complicated, it was still my anchor.

The Taylor household was my first community, my first lesson in love, loyalty, conflict, and survival. It was the foundation upon which everything else would be built; cracks and all.

My Father: Strength, Struggle, and "Miss Ann"

My father, Edward Taylor, was a man you noticed without needing an introduction. His laugh filled rooms before he even stepped inside. It was loud and infectious, the kind of laugh that made strangers smile even if they didn't know what was funny. He worked tirelessly, his hands roughened by labor, his back bent from years of carrying weight that wasn't just physical.

He loved playing cards, especially a game he called Beat the Devil, which he could play for hours all by himself. He also played checkers; cheating with a grin so wide you almost forgave him. Almost. He'd slide pieces when he thought you weren't looking, then deny it to the very end, his eyes sparkling with mischief.

"Daddy, you're cheating!" one of us would shout. "Who, me?" he'd say, leaning back with his hands raised in mock innocence. "Now why would I do a thing like that?"

But he also wrestled with demons.

Alcohol lingered nearby like an unwelcome guest who overstayed its welcome and slowly made itself at home. What began as a beer after work or a drink with friends grew into something heavier. The man who laughed so loudly began to shout even louder. The hands that once lifted us into the air sometimes slammed doors instead. The father who told stories became a man who forgot what he'd said the night before.

Still, even through exhaustion and alcohol, there were moments when his love broke through; quiet moments, familiar ones, moments that mattered.

To him, I was Miss Ann.

"Oh Lord, here comes Miss Ann," he'd say, laughing as I walked into the room with my hands on my hips, ready to tell someone what they should be doing.

"Why do you call me that, Daddy?"

"Because you're bossy and nosey," he'd say with a laugh. "Always telling folks what to do, how to do it, and when to do it. That's why I call you Miss Ann. That name comes from the South, the little lady sitting on the porch, minding everyone's business."

He'd take a sip of his Thunderbird; the cheap wine that always seemed within reach, and sometimes, after too many sips, his tone would shift.

"Get out my face, Miss Ann," he'd bark, waving me away.

Even then, the nickname held warmth. Miss Ann meant I was seen. It meant I had a voice, even before I knew how to use it. In his flawed, imperfect way, my father noticed me.

In September 1998, my father was diagnosed with terminal colon cancer. When the doctor shared the news, Daddy wasn't afraid, not even for a moment. He looked straight at him and asked, "Does that mean I'm going to kick the bucket?"

The doctor paused, unsure how to respond. Daddy didn't wait long.

"I'll ask it straight," he said. "Does that mean I'm going to die?"

The doctor answered quietly, "Unfortunately… within six months."

Daddy turned to my cousin and said, "Give me a cigarette." Once again, the doctor looked stunned. My cousin didn't miss a beat. "You just told this man he's going to die," she said. "Let him smoke."

That was Daddy; direct, unshaken, unwilling to sit with fear for too long. Even facing death, he refused to let it steal his power or his spirit.

He underwent minor colon surgery, and when I picked him up from the hospital, he said as he climbed into the car, "I'm not coming back here unless I'm in a body bag." He wasn't joking. He meant it.

As the weeks passed, cancer took him piece by piece; his strength, his appetite, his independence. Watching him fade broke something inside me that I didn't know it could break. The man who once filled rooms with laughter grew quiet and small. The hands that cheated at checkers struggled to hold a glass of water. The voice that called me Miss Ann faded into a whisper.

While I was out celebrating my birthday, my cousin called to say my father was possibly dying and refusing to go to the hospital. I rushed home, my celebration dissolving into dread. When I arrived, flashing ambulance lights painted the house in red and blue, shadows stretching across the walls. The family crowded his room, pleading with him to go, but in true stubborn fashion, he refused.

When he saw me, he said, "Oh Lord, here comes Miss Ann."

I begged him to go, my voice trembling. He still refused. The paramedics explained they couldn't force him, he was answering their questions clearly. Daddy just wanted to watch the baseball game, the sound low in the background, and be left alone.

They kept asking questions, and slowly confusion crept in. That was when the decision was made that he needed to go to the hospital. As the paramedics prepared to take him, he looked at them and said, "Please don't cut my pants." As they continued, he said "no" three times. Those were the last words I ever heard my father speak.

The ride to the hospital felt endless. I sat in the passenger seat of the ambulance, staring ahead, trying to catch a breath I couldn't quite find. He wasn't pronounced dead at the house; that would come later, at the hospital. Between the wail of the sirens and the unnatural stillness inside the ambulance, something inside me already knew. I didn't need anyone to tell me; the fear had settled like a stone in my chest.

When we arrived, they immediately rushed him to the back. Minutes later, we were led into a small room, and the doctor came in with quiet gravity. "Unfortunately," he said, "he didn't make it." My heart dropped, and I felt the weight of my family's disbelief pressing down on me. Daddy was gone.

We were allowed to see him. He looked peaceful, the pain finally gone, and for the first time in years, I imagined him with Mommy again, together at last. I traced the lines of his face, the hands that had once lifted me, that had cheated at checkers with a mischievous grin. He lay still, but every line, every feature, every breath of him still felt unmistakably Daddy.

And then I remembered the ride; the anticipation, the helplessness, the endless moments trapped between hope and fear. That ambulance ride would haunt me forever, a quiet witness to the moment of his passing.

On October 17, 1998—my 30th birthday, my father took his final breath. He died on the same day I was born, a date forever holding both celebration and loss, where life and death quietly met.

For years, birthdays felt heavy. Candles became markers of grief. Singing "Happy Birthday" felt dishonest. How could joy exist on the same day I lost him?

Now, decades later, I choose to remember his laughter. His stories. The way he called me Miss Ann and made me feel like I mattered, even when he couldn't show it the way I needed.

Even with all his flaws, he gave me strength. He taught me that people are complicated, that love doesn't always arrive neatly, and that forgiveness is something you do for yourself.

I believe he's watching now, somewhere beyond the pain, beyond the Thunderbird, beyond the regrets. I imagine him smiling, nodding, saying, "That's my girl."

Even though he couldn't give me everything I needed, he gave me enough to survive.

My Mother: The Glue That Held Us Together

If my father was strength wrapped in struggle, my mother, Addie Mae Taylor, was boldness wrapped in grace.

Where he was loud, she was unwavering. Where he wrestled with demons, she shouldered responsibility with hands that were worn but never still. Where he filled rooms with noise, she filled them with conviction, the kind that spoke volumes without needing to raise her voice.

Her smile could soften the hardest days. She worked endlessly, stretching every dollar until it screamed, feeding every mouth even when the cupboards looked bare, praying every night on her knees beside a bed crowded with worry.

She was the first one awake and the last one to sleep. Her hands were always busy; cooking, cleaning, mending, holding. She carried the family on her back with a strength that looked effortless but cost her everything.

She was the first to call me beautiful.

I remember the day clearly. I came home from school in tears, my glasses fogged, my heart bruised from another round of teasing. "Grandma Dynamite! Four eyes! Ugly!" Their laughter followed me home like a shadow I couldn't outrun.

I burst through the door, ran to my room, and collapsed onto the bed, sobbing into my pillow.

My mother came in quietly. She didn't ask what happened, she already knew. She sat beside me, her hand warm on my back.

"Crystal, you're beautiful," she said. "Don't ever let them tell you differently. God doesn't make mistakes."

She lifted my chin, so I had to look at her. "You hear me, baby? God. Doesn't. Make. Mistakes. You are exactly who you're supposed to be."

Those words became my anchor.

I came home from school like I always did; to drop off my books and then head to see my mother, who had been taken to the hospital a week earlier. She had struggled with heart disease for some time, so hospital visits were nothing new. She always came home. She was always okay.

This time was different.

Her heart was badly damaged, and she wasn't doing well. Still, I held on to hope. I just wanted her to know that I was there, that I missed her, that I loved her.

When I walked into the house on Tuesday, November 7, 1983, I was met on the steps by my cousin. Before I could say a word, she told me my mother, Addie Mae Taylor, had died.

My world stopped.

I collapsed into my cousin's arms, crying, repeating that it couldn't be true, that this wasn't real. But it was. From that moment on, life as I knew it was gone.

I was fifteen years old. My mother was only forty-five.

Losing her didn't just break my heart, it shattered my world. I lost my safe place, my shelter, my steady voice. Grief aged me. It forced me to grow far too soon.

Yet even in death, her lessons remained: strength in silence, power in words, faith as a foundation, and love as a legacy.

She is still the voice in my head whispering, *"Crystal, you're beautiful."*

And now, I believe her.

My Siblings

Growing up with seven siblings meant never being alone, but rarely being at peace.

Each of them shaped me in ways I didn't understand until much later. Some with love. Some with lessons. Some with pain that taught me what I would never tolerate in my own life.

Bruce, the oldest, was hard for me to love.

His harshness cut deep. His words were sharp, his presence heavy. I spent years wishing he would protect me, stand up for me, be the big brother I saw in movies. But he never was. And that absence taught me something crucial: that family titles don't guarantee love, and blood doesn't always mean safety.

From **Bruce**, I learned the value of boundaries. I learned that you can love someone from a distance. I learned that sometimes the people who hurt you the most are the ones you're supposed to be able to trust the most.

Calvin, unpredictable and volatile, reminded me that love does not mean accepting mistreatment.

There were moments of kindness from him, brief flashes of the brother I wished he could be. But those moments were always followed by cruelty: words that stung, betrayals that left scars. From him, I learned that patterns repeat unless someone chooses to break them.

William, quiet and strong, showed me that presence can speak louder than words.

He didn't say much, but when he was there, you felt it. His silence wasn't cold; it was steady. From him, I learned that strength doesn't always roar. Sometimes it's quiet, consistent, and reliable.

Peter, unique and mysterious, taught me that miracles come even after years of struggle from kidney disease.

He walked a hard road, faced rejection, and carried pain. But he found love eventually: real, lasting love. From him, I learned that your beginning doesn't dictate your ending.

Marcus, the jokester, showed me that humor can be survival.

He laughed through the pain, made jokes when things got heavy, lightened rooms that felt too dark. From him, I learned that laughter isn't denial; it's endurance.

Barry, the quiet one, reminded me that gentle hearts still leave deep marks.

He didn't demand attention. He didn't need the spotlight, but his kindness mattered. His presence mattered. From him, I learned that you don't have to be loud to be important.

Marie, the baby, survived her own storms (including being shot) and showed me what resilience truly looks like.

She faced trauma that would have destroyed others and came out still standing. From her, I learned that survival is a choice you make every single day.

My siblings were both my challenge and my classroom. Through them, I learned loyalty, loss, forgiveness, and the complicated truth that family is messy, imperfect, and sometimes painful, but it's also where we learn who we are and who we refuse to become.

Extended Family & Summers in Georgia

Our extended family was large and loud: a village of cousins, aunts, uncles, and people we called family even if we couldn't trace the exact bloodline.

Summers meant cookouts that stretched from afternoon into night. The air smelled of ribs on the grill, smoke curling into the sky, and collard greens simmering in big pots on makeshift tables. Music by Al Green and Aretha Franklin drifted through the humid air while children ran barefoot through the grass, playing tag until the mosquitoes came out.

Adults sat in lawn chairs, fanning themselves with folded paper plates, telling stories that got louder and more exaggerated with every beer. Laughter rose and fell like waves, and for a moment, everything felt right with the world.

But not every moment was kind.

Some cousins teased me until I cried, turning my joy into something small and shameful. Their laughter followed me like the mosquitoes: persistent, stinging, impossible to escape. They didn't know (or maybe they didn't care) how deep their words cut.

Those moments taught me that cruelty doesn't always come from strangers. Sometimes it comes from the people who are supposed to love you.

Yet Georgia held peace, too, especially at Grandma Bertha's house.

Her home was a sanctuary. Inside, the air smelled like peanut butter cake cooling on the counter and Pine-Sol on freshly mopped floors.

Grandma Bertha's hugs felt like healing. Her hands, wrinkled and soft, always found mine when I needed comfort. She didn't ask questions when I showed up quiet and withdrawn. She just made me a plate, sat me down, and let me be.

Even when the world outside was frightening (like during the Atlanta child murders that hung over the South like a dark cloud), her home felt safe. She prayed over us every night, her voice low and steady, asking God to protect her babies.

Those summers taught me resilience, faith, and the beauty of simple love. They taught me that peace can exist even in the middle of chaos, that joy can be found even when surrounded by pain.

They taught me that home isn't always a place. Sometimes it's a person.

Reflection: Breaking Cycles

Your bloodline shapes you, but it does not define your ending. Take a moment to reflect on what you've learned from your family's patterns; the love, pain, resilience, and the lessons they've imparted. Consider:

- Which traits or behaviors have been passed down that no longer serve you?

- Which moments of strength or love have shaped who you are today?

- How have experiences of loss, grief, or hardship taught you resilience?

- What patterns do you recognize, and which will you consciously choose to end?

Call to Action: Build a Legacy of Peace

The power to break cycles lies within you. Choose the path of conscious living, healing, and love.

1. **Acknowledge patterns** that no longer serve you. Name them. See them clearly.

2. **Decide what to keep.** Not everything from your past needs to be released; some of it is gold.

3. **Speak your truth.** Declare what you will no longer tolerate and what you are building instead.

4. **Forgive for your own freedom,** not to excuse others. Release the weight you've carried.

5. **Create new traditions** of peace, healing, and authenticity. Start today, no matter how small.

Reflective Journal Prompts

Use this space to look inward and write from your heart:

1. What traits or behaviors have I inherited that I want to release?

2. Who in my family demonstrated resilience, even without saying a word?

3. When have I felt unseen or unheard within my family? What truth do I need to tell myself about that moment?

4. How does "peace over pain" show up in my daily life?

5. What intentional actions will I take to build a future different from my past?

Write honestly. Cry if you need to. Rage if necessary. Then close your journal with this truth:

Final Affirmation: Choosing Peace

I am breaking generational patterns and choosing peace over pain. My past built me, but it will not bind me. I carry love, strength, resilience, faith, and boldness forward. I honor my bloodline, but I am the author of my own legacy.

CHAPTER 2

THROUGH THE EYES
BEHIND THE GLASSES

Affirmation: *I am no longer defined by ridicule. I am rising above every name that tried to break me.*

The Day My World Changed

Seventh grade felt like hope wrapped in new possibilities.

I couldn't wait to see my old friends again, to reconnect with familiar faces, and maybe, just maybe, to meet new ones who would accept me. I loved everything about the anticipation of this school year: my own locker with a combination lock that made me feel grown, changing classes like the high schoolers did, and the sense that I was finally stepping into a new version of myself.

But the moment that made me happiest was walking into science class and seeing that my cousin was there too.

My heart lifted. Thank God. It made me feel safe. Comforted. Protected. Our last names were close in the alphabet: "T" and "R." So, when the teacher announced he would seat us in alphabetical order, I thought, *"Good, I'll be close to my cousin."*

And I was.

For a brief, beautiful moment, I believed I wouldn't be alone. I had no idea how wrong that belief was.

The Alphabet Changed Everything

The science teacher stood at the front of the classroom with a clipboard, calling names in alphabetical order. His voice was monotone, bored; like he'd done this a hundred times before and would do it a hundred times more.

"Taylor." I stood, my heart beating a little faster, and walked to the seat he pointed to, right next to the jokesters. The kids who could turn cruelty into comedy. The ones whose laughter carried power, whose jokes landed because people were afraid not to laugh. I sat down quietly, shrinking myself, hoping I could disappear.

A few names later, the teacher called my cousin. I was placed close to him, just as I expected. Relief washed over me. I looked at him, my eyes silently saying: *Good. If they start something, at least you're here.*

But when the teasing began; the looks, the pointing, the whispers that weren't quite whispers, something in him shifted. He didn't laugh with them. But he didn't defend me either. He stared straight ahead, jaw clenched, pretending I didn't exist. I could feel his embarrassment radiating off him, not because he didn't care about me, but because he didn't want their attention to turn on him too. That hurt. It hurt more than the jokes, more than the stares. Because at that moment, I realized something devastating: even the people you believe will protect you sometimes choose their own safety over yours.

Later that day, he went home and told the family what happened in class, not to protect me, not to ask how to help, but because he was embarrassed to be associated with me. That cut deeper than anything the boys ever said.

The Birth of "Grandma Dynamite"

The nickname came quickly. One of the jokesters leaned over, squinting through exaggerated gestures, mocking the way my thick glasses magnified my eyes.

"Look at her; she looks like Grandma Dynamite from *The Flintstones!*"

Laughter exploded. "Yeah! That's it!" "Grandma Dynamite!"

The name stuck; loud, cruel, unforgettable. By the end of the week, kids I'd never spoken to knew it. Strangers in the hallway shouted at me. Fingers pointed. Laughter followed. I wanted to disappear. Every morning, I woke up hoping it would stop. Hoping someone would forget. Hoping I could just be Jennifer, the girl who loved science, who wanted friends, who wanted to belong.

But the name followed me everywhere, like a shadow I couldn't outrun.

Wanting to Belong

All I ever wanted was simple, achingly simple. One real friend. One safe place to sit at lunch. One person to say, "Leave her alone."

I changed my hair. I spoke less. I learned how to smile through pain. I swallowed the hurt and buried it where no one could see. Every night, I cried into my pillow, hoping tomorrow would be different; hoping someone would see me as more than a joke. Hoping I wouldn't have to brace myself before walking into a room.

But tomorrow always looks like today. What I didn't know then was that the very pain meant to break me was shaping me, building something I couldn't see yet: resilience, strength, a voice that would one day rise above cruelty. That little girl hiding behind thick glasses would survive.

The Day Everything Shifted

Then everything changed in a way none of us could have imagined. On Tuesday, December 16, 1980, my cousin, the same boy who sat near me in science class, was shot and killed by his friend. He was only fourteen years old. Just a kid. Just beginning to grow into himself. Just learning how to navigate the world, its pressures, its expectations.

One day he was beside me in school, trying to protect himself from ridicule. The next day, he was gone.

The news hit our family like a tidal wave. Phones rang through the night. Conversations collapsed into sobs. Grief filled the heavy, suffocating, unfamiliar air. This was the first time our family had ever experienced death, and especially the death of a child. Nothing prepares you for that kind of loss.

At school, everything shifted. The teasing softened. The laughter faded. Teachers spoke to me differently, their voices gentler, their eyes more careful. The halls felt quieter, heavier, filled with something like guilt. Most people hadn't even known we were related until that day. But once the news spread, everything changed. For a moment, just a moment, I could breathe.

But the nickname didn't disappear. By then, it was everywhere, school, home, the neighborhood. No matter where I went, someone was calling me "Grandma Dynamite." It had become part of my identity, whether I wanted it or not. And in a twisted way, my cousin's death became the only thing that gave me temporary relief, not because people suddenly cared, but because laughing at me felt uncomfortable now. Grief became my shield. A shield I never wanted.

A Powerful Closing

His life was brief, and his death was brutal, but the mark he left on me is enduring. Losing him taught me the fragility of life, the weight of grief, and the courage it takes to keep standing when the world feels unkind. In surviving the pain, I carry pieces of him: his laughter, his presence, and the reminder that even in the darkest moments, resilience is possible.

I became stronger because of him, and though he isn't here to see it, his memory lives on in every act of courage, every voice raised against injustice, and every heart that refuses to be broken.

The Weight of Silence

There's a special kind of loneliness that comes with being bullied.

It's not just the teasing itself. It's the silence that surrounds it, the way adults don't notice, or worse, notice but do nothing. The way other kids look away, grateful it's not them. The way you learn to carry it all alone because telling someone feels more dangerous than staying quiet.

I wanted to tell my mother. But she was already carrying so much. How could I add to her burden?

I wanted to tell my father. But he was lost in his own struggles, his own fog. Would he even hear me?

I wanted to tell a teacher. But what would they do? Tell the kids to stop? That would only make it worse.

So, I stayed silent.

Silence became my survival strategy. If I didn't talk about it, maybe it wasn't real. If I pretended it didn't hurt, maybe eventually it wouldn't.

But silence is a thief. It steals your voice, your confidence, your belief that anyone cares. It teaches you that your pain doesn't matter, that you don't matter.

And for years, I believed that lie.

The Cousin Who Didn't Protect Me

I think about my cousin often. The one who sat beside me in science class. The one who knew what was happening but chose his own comfort over my protection.

For a long time, I was angry at him.

How could you just sit there? How could you pretend you didn't know me? How could you go home and complain about being embarrassed instead of standing up for me?

But as I've grown older, I've come to understand something painful and true: fear makes people do things they regret. Fear of being laughed at. Fear of becoming the target. Fear of losing their own fragile sense of belonging.

He was just a kid, too; a kid trying to survive in middle school, trying to fit in, trying not to drown in the same waters I was drowning in.

His death stole any chance I had to tell him I understood. To tell him I forgave him. To tell him that even though he didn't protect me, I still loved him.

And now, all I can do is carry the lesson his life and death taught me: when you have the chance to stand up for someone, do it. You might not get another chance.

What Bullying Really Does

People who haven't been bullied often think it's just words. Just kids being kids. Just something you get over.

But bullying doesn't just hurt in the moment. It reshapes how you see yourself.

It teaches you that something is wrong with you. That you're too much or not enough. That you deserve cruelty because there must be something about you that invites it.

It makes you hyper-focused on your flaws. Every morning, I stared at my glasses in the mirror, hating them, wishing I could see without them, wishing I could be normal.

It makes you invisible in the worst way. You want to disappear to escape the teasing, but you also desperately want to be seen, truly seen, for who you are beneath the surface.

And it plants seeds of shame that grow for years. Even now, decades later, there are moments when I hear laughter behind me and my body tenses. Moments when I wonder if people are laughing at me.

Bullying leaves scars you can't see. But they're real. And they last.

The Strength I Didn't Know I Had

But here's what I also know now, something I couldn't see then: I survived.

Every day I walked back into that school, I was brave.

Every night I cried and still woke up the next morning, I was being strong.

Every time I swallowed the hurt and kept moving forward, I was building the foundation for the woman I would become.

I didn't feel strong. I felt broken. But strength isn't about feeling powerful. It's about showing up even when you feel powerless.

And I showed up. Every single day.

That little girl with the thick glasses, the one they called Grandma Dynamite, the one who wanted to disappear, didn't give up.

She kept going.

And that? That was everything.

Call to Action: Stand Up for the Child You Once Were

Take a moment right now to think about your younger self. The one who wanted safety and acceptance. The one who felt unseen, unprotected, unheard.

Promise that child something:

- Promise them you will speak up now, for yourself and for others.

- Promise them you will be the protector they didn't have.

- Promise them you will walk boldly, loudly, and proudly from this day forward.

- Promise them their pain was not in vain, that it built something beautiful inside you.

Write that promise down. Say it out loud. Let it be your commitment to healing.

You survived for a reason; now it's time to rise.

Reflection Questions

Take time to sit with these questions. Write honestly. Feel deeply.

1. What moment in your childhood made you feel unprotected?

2. Who were you hoping would stand up for you, and how did it feel when they didn't?

3. What name, label, or insult followed you longer than it should have?

4. If you could talk to your seventh-grade self, what would you tell her now?

5. How did grief or loss change the way people treated you?

Final Affirmation

Say this out loud, with your hand on your heart: Even when they didn't protect me, I survived. Even when the laughter followed me, I kept going. And today, I walk boldly with the confidence I once prayed for.

CHAPTER 3

FROM THE PORCH TO PURPOSE: BUILDING INDEPENDENCE AFTER LIFE CHANGED

Affirmation: *Even when life didn't give me the path I dreamed of, I created my own road and kept walking forward.*

Joy Before the Silence

June 1985: I had just finished my junior year of high school. Standing on the threshold of senior year, I felt a thrill I had never known before. After everything I had endured, I was finally at the finish line. That summer, I worked long hours, counting every dollar, dreaming of fresh clothes and a new start.

Then came the trip. Our family piled into the car, the air buzzing with laughter and excitement as we drove to an amusement park in New Jersey. The sun sparkled on the rides, the air smelled of popcorn and cotton candy, and the screams of thrill-seekers mingled with our own. Aunt Betty, my mother's youngest sister, was there with us, laughing, holding on tight on roller coasters, sharing in every twist and turn. I could still hear her voice ringing out, pure and joyous, as we raced from ride to ride.

That night, we drove home with cheeks sore from smiling, our voices full of stories and laughter. I went to bed thinking it had been one of the best days of my life.

The next morning, the world fell apart. Aunt Betty had been rushed to the hospital. The news was unreal, like a bad dream. Days later, on Wednesday, August 7, 1985, she was gone. Just like that, the laughter vanished. She had been like a second mother to me, and suddenly, the world felt hollow, cruel, and silent. How could someone I had been laughing with just yesterday be gone forever?

School started, and life moved on. I ate in the senior lunchroom, took graduation pictures, felt a sense of belonging I had never felt before. But behind every smile, there was a shadow. I never went to prom, never experienced those carefree nights my friends had. Still, I was graduating, stepping forward into a future that demanded I carry both the joy of memories and the weight of loss. Somehow, that was enough to keep going.

June 1986: Graduation day.

The air buzzed with excitement as families filled the football field, cameras flashing, flowers being handed over with hugs and tears. Proud parents stood on tiptoes trying to get the perfect shot. Siblings waved homemade signs. Grandparents dabbed their eyes with tissues.

When my name was called, "Jennifer Taylor," I walked across that stage with my head held high, my cap slightly crooked, my heart pounding with a mix of pride and loneliness.

I was the only Taylor child to graduate high school. The first. The only.

That should have meant something. That should have been celebrated. But while my classmates were surrounded by cameras, congratulations, and bouquets of flowers, I went home to a quiet porch and whispered to myself, "You did it."

No party. No cake. No family gathered around telling me how proud they were.

Just me, my cap and gown, and the creaking wooden boards of the porch that had held me through so many silent tears.

That porch became my stage, the place where I learned one of life's hardest but most important lessons: if no one celebrates you, celebrate yourself.

I sat there for a long time that evening, still wearing my gown, watching the sun set over Mount Vernon. I let myself feel the sadness of what wasn't there. But I also let myself feel the pride of what I had accomplished.

I graduated. Against the odds. Against the grief of losing my mother. Against the bullying that tried to convince me I wasn't smart enough. Against a family system that didn't prioritize education.

I did it anyway.

That night marked the beginning of my independence. Not because I chose it, but because I had to claim it.

Dreams Denied, A New Path Forced

College was supposed to be my next step. My escape. My freedom. I had dreams of walking across a campus, books tucked under my arm, joining clubs, making friends who didn't know me as "Grandma Dynamite." I dreamed of late-night study sessions, football games, dorm rooms decorated with posters and fairy lights. I dreamed of becoming more than my circumstances. But when I told my aunt about my plans, her response was swift and final.

"You can't go to college." The words hit me like a slap. "What do you mean I can't go?" "We don't have the money, Crystal. You need to get a job. You need to help out." I stood there, stunned. The door I thought was open had just slammed shut before I could even knock. I cried that night. Hard. The kind of crying that shakes your whole body and leaves you exhausted.

But somewhere between the tears and the sunrise, I decided: if no one was going to open a path for me, I would create my own. College wasn't an option right now. Fine. But giving up wasn't an option either. I would like to find another way. I always did.

The Youth Program: My First Lesson in Adulthood

I entered a youth employment program shortly after graduation. It wasn't glamorous. It wasn't what I had envisioned for myself. But it was something.

I filed papers into dusty office cabinets. I swept floors. I answered phones. I made copies. I ran errands for people who barely looked at me when they gave me instructions.

At first, it felt beneath me. I had just graduated from high school, and I wanted to be doing something important, something meaningful.

But over time, I learned something crucial: every task teaches you something if you're willing to pay attention.

Filing papers taught me organization and attention to detail. Sweeping floors taught me that no job is beneath you if it's honest work. Answering phones taught me how to speak professionally, how to handle difficult people, and how to stay calm under pressure. Running errands taught me the layout of the city, how to navigate public transportation, and how to manage my time.

My first paycheck wasn't much. But when I held it in my hands, I felt something I hadn't felt in a long time: pride.

This was mine. I earned this; no one gave it to me and no one could take it away.

Every task, no matter how small, became a lesson. Every day taught me something school never could; how to survive, how to show up, and how to prove my worth through consistency and effort.

The Temp Agency: Learning to Adapt

After the youth program ended, I joined a temp agency. My life became a series of short-term assignments, each one in a different office, with different people, different expectations, different environments.

I was assigned to a large pharmaceutical company, surrounded by people in crisp lab coats and tailored suits, discussing projects and protocols I was still learning to navigate. The smell of coffee filled the office, and even though I was the youngest person there, I felt like an adult; responsible, seen, and part of something bigger than myself.

Technically, I was a temporary staff member, but I didn't let that limit me. I learned to observe; how successful people carried themselves, how they spoke, how they handled conflict. I adapted quickly, learned new skills on the spot, and made myself indispensable, even in a short amount of time. Being underestimated became my advantage. I exceeded expectations and, despite the obstacles placed before me, rose to the occasion and proved my value in every assignment.

When that assignment came to an end, I was deeply disappointed. I had poured my heart into the work and hoped it would last longer. I was down for a moment, but I refused to stay there.

I took a deep breath, squared my shoulders, and reminded myself: keep smiling, keep moving, keep going. I called the temp agency, and before I knew it, I was heading to my next assignment, ready to prove myself all over again.

Finding Purpose at the Greenvale Police Department

In 1986, the temp agency sent me to the Town of Greenvale Police Department.

I thought it was just another temporary placement. Another few weeks, maybe a month, and then I'd be sent somewhere else.

But when I walked through those doors for the first time, something in my spirit said, "You're home."

I didn't understand it at first. The police department didn't seem like the kind of place where I belonged. I wasn't a cop. I couldn't be a cop; my eyesight wouldn't allow it. The thick glasses that had made me a target my whole life had also closed certain doors.

But my uncle had served as a detective there. His legacy lived in those halls, and even though I couldn't wear the badge, I decided I could serve in my own way.

I treated every assignment like it mattered, because it did.

I typed reports with precision, making sure every detail was accurate. I filed documents carefully, knowing that someone's case might depend on finding that paperwork quickly. I answered phones professionally, understanding that the voice on the other end might be someone in crisis.

I showed up early. I stayed late when needed. I volunteered for tasks others didn't want to do.

And slowly, quietly, I built a reputation for being reliable, thorough, and deeply invested in my work.

By May 1987, the "temporary" job was no longer temporary, it had become a full-time position, a career, and a place where I felt I belonged.

What started as just another assignment became a decades-long journey. A purpose. A home.

Facing Workplace Bullying: Grown-Up Cruelty

I once thought bullying ended after school. Once you became an adult, people grew up and cruelty stopped.

I was wrong. Bullying doesn't end; it just changes uniforms.

At the police department, the teasing about my glasses resurfaced. I remember someone saying to me, "Those are thick, they look like Coke bottles." I heard whispers and laughter, the kind that follows you even when you try to pretend you don't notice. Jokes I wasn't supposed to hear still found their way to me, lingering longer than they should have. I wanted to disappear in that moment, to shrink myself until I was invisible. Instead, I forced a smile, turned away, and walked off, carrying the shame with me in silence, pretending it didn't hurt while feeling every bit of it.

The same pain from childhood returned, dressed in professional clothing, hiding behind polite smiles and passive-aggressive comments.

But this time, *I* was different.

I would cry in the bathroom and come out with a smile on my face. I didn't have the luxury of crying and then going home to my mother anymore; my mother was gone. I was an adult now, with bills to pay and responsibilities that didn't pause grief or exhaustion. There was no safe place to fall apart, no one to carry the weight for me. So, I learned to wipe my tears, straighten my posture, and keep moving. I showed up even when my heart felt heavy, because showing up was no longer a choice, it was survival.

So, I made a choice: I would let my work speak for me.

Every report I typed, I did with precision and care. Every task I completed, I did with excellence. Every phone call I answered, I handled it with professionalism.

My consistency became my quiet defiance.

There were still days I escaped to the bathroom to cry, whispering prayers through tears: "God, give me strength. Help me get through this day."

But I never stopped showing up. I never gave them the satisfaction of seeing me break. I never let them make me quit.

I had learned something powerful by then: the best response to doubt is excellence. The best response to gossip is consistency. The best response to cruelty is refusing to become cruel yourself.

Balancing Family, Grief, and Responsibility

Adulthood came fast. Too fast.

My mother's death had already forced me into caretaking, long before I was ready. Even though I worked full-time at the police department, even as I tried to build my own life, I was still the one everyone leaned on.

Financially. Emotionally. Spiritually.

There were days I gave my last dollar to a family member who needed it more and nights I stayed up comforting someone else while holding my own pain in silence. In the mornings I woke up exhausted but still showed up because people were counting on me.

Independence came with a cost: the weight of responsibility that no one asked if I could carry.

But it also came with power: the knowledge that I *could* carry it. I was strong enough. I didn't need anyone to save me because I had learned how to save myself.

Becoming Independent: Learning to Stand Tall

Working full-time at eighteen taught me a truth I carry to this day: no one was coming to save me.

Not my family. Not a fairy godmother. Not a miracle.

If I wanted a different life, I had to build it myself. One paycheck at a time. One decision at a time. One day at a time.

Bills didn't care that I was grieving. Rent didn't wait for me to feel ready. Responsibility didn't pause because I was tired.

So, I learned to stand tall even when I wanted to crumble.

I stopped waiting for applause and started clapping for myself.

I celebrated small victories that no one else would notice: paying rent on time, keeping food in the fridge, choosing peace over anger, getting out of bed on the hardest mornings.

Each quiet triumph became another brick in the foundation of my resilience.

I learned that independence isn't about not needing anyone. It's about knowing you can survive even when help doesn't come. It's about building a life on your own terms, even when the path wasn't the one you dreamed of.

Reflections: Turning Rejection into Resilience

Looking back now, I see that rejection wasn't punishment. It was redirection.

Every "no" I received built the strength I needed to handle life ahead. Every closed door forced me to find a window. Every disappointment taught me to create my own opportunities.

I didn't get to go to college right away. But I got an education in resilience, adaptability, and perseverance that no classroom could have taught me.

I didn't get the celebration I wanted at graduation. But I learned to celebrate myself, a skill that would serve me throughout my life.

I didn't get the easy path, but I got something better: the knowledge that I could walk the hard path and come out stronger on the other side.

I wasn't just surviving anymore. I was building something lasting: a career, a sense of purpose, a deep understanding of who I was and what I was capable of.

Call to Action: Create Your Own Road

Rejection is not the end, it's the beginning of your custom-made path.

You don't need permission to start. You don't need perfect circumstances. You don't need someone else to believe in you before you believe in yourself.

Start where you are. Build what you can. Believe in what's inside you.

Here's your challenge:

1. Revisit a dream someone told you was "too big." Take one small step toward it today. Just one.

2. Replace every lie you've been told with a truth that uplifts you. Write it down. Say it out loud.

3. Write down the ways rejection has shaped your resilience; not to dwell on pain, but to recognize growth.

4. Decide that even if no one claps, you'll keep going. You are the architect of your destiny, and the road you build will lead you further than any open door ever could.

Reflective Journal: Walking Your Own Path

Take time to write honestly:

1. When was the last time you felt overlooked or uncelebrated? How did you handle it?

2. What's one door that closed, and what new direction did it push you toward?

3. How can you celebrate yourself in small, meaningful ways this week?

4. What lessons have work, responsibility, or hardship taught you about independence?

5. Finish this sentence: Even when life told me no, I decided to...

Final Affirmation

Say this with conviction:

Even when life didn't give me the path I dreamed of, I created my own road and kept walking forward. I am not a victim of my circumstances. I am the architect of my future. And I will keep building, one step at a time.

CHAPTER 4

THE PAIN I CARRIED, THE STRENGTH I BECAME

Affirmation: *Even when I was hurting, I kept moving. Even when I was silent, I was surviving.*

Carrying Pain in Silence

For most of my life, I became an expert at hiding pain.

I knew how to show up with a smile even when my heart was breaking. I knew how to laugh at jokes even when nothing felt funny. I knew how to say "I'm fine" with such conviction that people believed me, even when I was drowning inside.

Pain became my second skin, always with me, always heavy, always hidden beneath layers of performance and pretense.

I carried the sting of childhood bullying, the weight of being called "Grandma Dynamite" until the nickname felt more real than my own name. I carried the ache of losing my mother too soon, of being fifteen and suddenly motherless in a world that didn't pause for my grief. I carried the loneliness of walking across a graduation stage with no one cheering from the stands, of celebrating milestones in silence.

But that pain was only the beginning.

As I stepped into adulthood, I entered relationships that promised love but delivered heartbreak. One of those relationships would eventually result in the birth of my son. What should have been comfort became chaos. What should have been tenderness became torment. What should have felt like home felt like a battlefield.

Behind closed doors, words cut deeper than knives ever could. Bruises, both seen and unseen, became my reality. The visible ones I could hide with long sleeves and makeup. The invisible ones, the ones carved into my spirit, were harder to conceal.

I told myself to stay strong. I told myself to keep quiet. I told myself that love required sacrifice, that relationships were hard work, that maybe if I just tried harder, loved better, gave more, things would change.

But silence became my prison. Every insult chipped away at my confidence until I barely recognized the woman in the mirror. Every betrayal added another layer of shame. Every broken promise taught me to stop believing in happy endings.

The Weight of Survival

There's a kind of exhaustion that survival brings. Not just physically, though that's part of it. But emotional, mental, and spiritual exhaustion that seeps into your bones and makes even breathing feel like effort.

You wake up tired. You go to bed tired. And still, you find the strength to pretend everything's okay because letting people see your pain feels more dangerous than carrying it alone.

Every morning, I put on my mask. I perfected the art of looking put together when I was falling apart. I smiled at coworkers who had no idea what my nights looked like. I laughed at family gatherings while swallowing screams. I said "I'm okay" when asked how I was doing, because the truth felt too heavy to speak out loud.

People didn't know the pain I carried home with me. To the outside world, they saw a strong woman, reliable Jennifer; the one who showed up, got things done, and never complained.

But I saw someone barely holding it together. Someone whose strength was really stubbornness, a refusal to let the world see her break.

The truth I learned later was this: **surviving isn't the same as living.**

I was surviving, but I wasn't living. I was enduring, but I wasn't thriving.

There's a difference between getting through the day and experiencing joy in the day, between breathing and truly being alive.

For years, I confused the two.

Setting the Stage for Change

Everything I carried (every insult, every betrayal, every silent tear, every moment I wanted to give up but didn't) was shaping me in ways I couldn't see yet.

I didn't know it then, but my pain was preparing me.

For a long time, I believed that strength meant never crying, never breaking, never admitting I was hurting. I thought strong women didn't need help. Strong women didn't fall apart. Strong women held everything together no matter what.

But I learned that true strength isn't born in the standing; it's born in the breaking.

True strength is admitting when you can't do it alone. True strength is asking for help. True strength is falling apart and trusting that you have what it takes to put yourself back together.

The pain I carried would one day become my strength, the same strength that helped me walk away from abuse, raise my son with love he'd never seen modeled, and rebuild my life from the ground up.

But first, I had to walk through the fire. And the fire was hotter than I ever imagined.

Living with Abuse: The Battles Behind Closed Doors

I met David's father one day while hanging out with my cousin. I remember thinking, *wow, this guy really wants to talk to me.* The warning signs were there, he was literally leaning out of the passenger side of his friend's car, but I chose to ignore them. We started to "date," and I felt happy; convinced I had finally found someone who would love me. I was wrong.

Not long after, I found out I was pregnant. I was nervous to tell him and terrified to tell my family. When I finally did, David was excited and even came with me to tell my aunt. At first, there was anger, but it slowly gave way to acceptance, especially knowing I had a stable income and was prepared to take responsibility for my child.

David Jr. was born on January 19, 1989, and I was overwhelmed with joy. I finally had someone who would love me unconditionally. But that joy didn't last long. Life quickly became a struggle. David Sr.'s behavior grew increasingly abusive, and he convinced me to leave my aunt's house and move in with him and his family. I believed it would be a fresh start, easy, even, but once again, I was wrong.

He refused to watch David Jr. while I worked, forcing me to find childcare. He quit his job, and I became responsible for not only my share of the rent, but his as well, paying his mother for both of us. David Sr. stayed out late, often not coming home at all. I worked full-time, attended college, and relied on public transportation to get everywhere, while he stayed home, doing nothing. Love should have felt safe.

Love should have felt like coming home after a long day, like finally exhaling after holding your breath, like being chosen again. But what I lived through was anything but safe.

At first, it was subtle, so subtle I nearly missed it. Sharp words disguised as jokes. *"I'm just playing, Crystal. Don't be so sensitive."* Control masked as concern. *"I'm just looking out for you. I don't want you to get hurt."*

Over time, the subtlety disappeared. What began as charm turned into manipulation. Compliments gave way to criticism. What felt like protection revealed itself as possession.

David Sr. convinced me that every argument was my fault. Every bruise, every cold shoulder, every stretch of silence was something I had caused; that if I just tried harder, spoke softer, gave more, things would get better.

I started to believe maybe I was the problem. Maybe I was too much, too loud, too emotional, too demanding. Or maybe I wasn't enough, not pretty enough, not patient enough, not supportive enough.

Some bruises faded in days, purple turning yellow before disappearing altogether. Others settled deep inside me, invisible but lasting, reshaping the way I saw myself and the way I moved through the world.

Emotional wounds leave no fingerprints, but they change everything; the way you hold your shoulders, the way you flinch at raised voices, the way you apologize for things that aren't your fault, the way you shrink just to keep the peace.

Silence as Survival

Silence became my armor and my cage.

If I didn't argue, maybe the storm would pass. If I stayed quiet, maybe the anger would fade. If I just agreed, maybe there would be peace, even if it was temporary, even if it was false.

Outsiders never saw it. They saw "strong Jennifer," the woman who worked full-time, raised her son, showed up for family, and never cracked.

No one knew that at night, I cried myself to sleep, praying for peace that never came. No one knew that I jumped at the sound of keys in the door, bracing myself for whatever mood I encountered. No one knew that I rehearsed conversations in my head, trying to predict which words would trigger anger and which might bring calm.

I feared judgment. I feared the whispers: "Why doesn't she just leave?" I feared the pity in people's eyes if they knew the truth. Most of all, I feared being asked the question I wasn't ready to answer: "Why are you still there?"

People didn't know the pain I carried home with me. To the outside world, they saw a strong woman, reliable Jennifer. The one who showed up, got things done, and never complained.

But I saw someone barely holding it together. Someone whose strength was really stubbornness, a refusal to let the world see her break.

The breaking came when the disrespect became impossible to ignore. One day, a young woman knocked on the door. That's when I learned the father of my child was trying to start a relationship with her. To justify himself, he told her I was on drugs. That was a blatant lie. He told her that he was the one taking care of our son, another lie. He even claimed the new clothes I had bought for our child were his doing. Even more lies.

The young woman wasn't cruel. She was respectful. She was kind. Somehow, she felt more empathy for me than the man who was supposed to love me. Her words, spoken gently, gave me the strength to leave, and never look back.

Because leaving wasn't simple. Leaving wasn't just walking out the door.

Leaving meant unlearning everything I thought love was supposed to be.

Leaving meant admitting I had made a mistake, that I had stayed too long, that I had ignored the red flags everyone else seemed to see.

Leaving meant facing the unknown, and sometimes the known, no matter how painful, feels safer than uncertainty.

One day, I gathered the courage to leave. Going back to my aunt's house meant choosing safety and choosing myself. I never looked back, and I have no regrets.

The Man I Met at the Mall: The Emotional Roller Coaster

His name was Michael, the man I met at the mall who took me on an emotional roller coaster I never saw coming. Our relationship moved very quickly. At first, he seemed charming and attentive, but beneath that charm was jealousy and control. Over time, the relationship became mentally, emotionally, verbally, and physically abusive. I covered up the abuse, wearing a mask around family, friends, and colleagues, pretending everything was fine while silently carrying the pain.

In the end, Michael left me for a young woman he had been involved with at his job. But before that end, there was a moment that stripped everything down to the truth.

On the day of my father's wake, I needed support more than ever before. I needed him to be present. I needed compassion and comfort during one of the hardest moments of my life. Instead, Michael told me he had to work, but that wasn't the truth. That was the day he chose to help a woman from his job move into her apartment.

I didn't learn this until the day after I buried my father, when she called my home and told me everything. Michael didn't deny it. That night marked the peak of the disrespect, the emotional, verbal, and physical harm escalated to its highest point.

The next morning, I went to work trying to hold myself together. There were no phone calls. No messages. No explanations. When I returned home, the silence made sense, Michael's belongings were gone.

I cried. I called. There was no response.

What I felt wasn't just heartbreak, it was shame, hurt, betrayal and deep disgust. That was the end of that relationship.

Abuse does not begin with chaos. It begins with predictable, cyclical, patterns that trap you before you realize you are caught.

First, the tension builds. You feel the air change. The silence thickens. You begin walking on eggshells, trying not to trigger what you sense is coming.

Then comes the explosion.

The insult.

The argument.

The slap.

The door slamming.

The words you can't unhear.

After that, the apology. Tears. Promises.

"I didn't mean it."

"It won't happen again."

"You know I love you."

Then the honeymoon phase. Brief peace. Laughter. Moments that remind you why you stayed, moments that convince you this time will be different.

But it never is.

The tension returns. The cycle repeats.

Each time, hope gets smaller.

Each time, fear grows larger.

Each time, peace feels harder to remember.

I was trapped in that loop, caught between who Michael appeared to be in the calm and who he became in the storm. I called it love because I didn't understand what love truly was.

Real love doesn't make you afraid.

Real love doesn't require you to shrink.

Real love doesn't leave bruises; visible or invisible.

But I didn't know that yet.

Carrying Pain at Work

Even as I suffered at home, I showed up at work.

I answered phones with a steady, professional voice. I smiled at coworkers who joked about their weekends, wondering what they would think if they knew how I had spent mine. I hid marks under long sleeves and high collars, careful with how I moved so no one would ask questions.

People teased me about being quiet. About being serious. About my thick glasses. They didn't know that laughter could trigger memories, that certain tones tightened my chest, that my silence was survival.

Some days, I escaped to the bathroom to cry. I locked the stall, covered my mouth to quiet the sobs, washed my face, straightened my posture, and returned to my desk as if nothing had happened.

That was my double life; the professional woman by day, the survivor by night.

And no one knew.

I had become very good at hiding.

The Turning Point: My Father's Funeral and Breaking the Cycle

The true turning point came with my father's funeral.

Grief has a way of cutting through denial. Standing there, saying goodbye to the man who raised me, I realized something I could no longer ignore. I could not continue surviving and still honor the life that shaped me.

The days surrounding his funeral brought everything into sharp focus: the absence of support, the emotional abandonment, the repeated harm I had learned to normalize. What once felt confusing suddenly felt undeniable.

The day after I buried my father, I received a phone call from the woman I had been abandoned for. She told me the truth about their relationship and about the day he said he was going to work, the day he was instead helping her move. He did not deny it.

That night became one of the hardest I ever endured. The emotional, verbal, and physical abuse escalated to its worst point, leaving me overwhelmed with grief, shock, and exhaustion. The next morning, I went to work trying to hold myself together, unaware that while I was fighting to function, he was quietly removing his belongings from our home.

When I returned, the silence told the story, he was gone.

In that moment, it felt like abandonment layered on top of unbearable loss. I cried. I called. There was no answer. Shame, hurt, and deep disgust settled in, and I believed I had been discarded at my most vulnerable.

With time, however, clarity replaced confusion. What felt like rejection was, in truth, release. His departure; though cruel in its timing, ended a cycle of abuse I had been struggling to escape. What I once saw as abandonment, I now recognize as the beginning of my freedom.

For the first time, I stopped asking, "What did I do wrong?" and began asking, "Why am I accepting this?"

That shift, became awareness, and the beginning of healing.

This is the message I later carried onto the TEDx stage: cycles continue when they go unnamed. Silence allows harm to repeat. Healing begins the moment we tell ourselves the truth.

Breaking the cycle didn't happen all at once. It began with recognition. With boundaries. With choosing peace over familiarity and safety over denial.

I didn't leave because I was fearless.

I became strong because staying was costing me too much.

My father's passing became more than a loss—it became a line in the sand. A reminder that life is fragile, time is not promised, and love should never require suffering to prove its worth.

That was the beginning of my becoming.

The Man with Dreadlocks: A Love That Drained Me

When you've been hurt deeply, even a broken kind of love can feel like relief. That's what drew me to Larry, the man with dreadlocks. Larry was charming, confident, and magnetic. His presence filled a room. When he walked in, people noticed. When he spoke, people listened. And when his attention was on me, I felt seen in a way I hadn't felt in years.

For a while, I convinced myself he was part of my healing, a balm for wounds I had been carrying for far too long. But charm can be a mask, and eventually, masks slip.

Whenever I tried to address concerns or speak honestly about our relationship, Larry dismissed them. He believed I was exaggerating, covering things up, or denying his perspective. Accountability was never part of the conversation. Everything cycled back to his needs, his priorities, his feelings. Over time, it became clear that Larry was deeply self-centered, unable, or unwilling, to consider how his behavior affected anyone but himself.

He didn't hurt me physically; there were no visible bruises this time. But the damage came in quieter ways, emotional exhaustion, mental strain, and spiritual depletion. Larry's affection was inconsistent, offered and withdrawn depending on his mood. One day attentive, the next distant. His promises were easy to make and impossible to keep. Words meant to hold me in place, not move us forward.

And still, I stayed.

As time passed, I realized the truth I had been avoiding: I was settling. Not because I didn't deserve more, but because I was afraid of starting over again. There was no real future for Larry and me, only a cycle of hoping, waiting, and disappointment. I told myself to be patient, to keep giving, to keep proving my worth. I believed that if I loved harder, supported more, and sacrificed enough, Larry would eventually see my value.

But love should not feel like begging. Love should not require constant self-erasure. Love should not leave you emptier than you were before.

Eventually, I reached a quiet but painful realization: I was tired of being the only one trying. Tired of shrinking so Larry could feel tall. Tired of pouring everything into a cup that never poured back.

When I looked at my son, David, something shifted. I knew I could not continue modeling a version of love rooted in imbalance and emotional neglect. I didn't want him believing that relationships were meant to drain you, or that love required losing yourself to keep someone else comfortable.

So, I made a quiet choice to walk away. That choice didn't come with applause or certainty, but it came with peace. And that choice became my liberation.

Lessons Learned

Larry taught me things I needed to learn, even if the lessons came wrapped in pain.

He taught me that not all abuse is physical. Sometimes it's emotional neglect, indifference, and inconsistency. Sometimes it's the absence of effort disguised as, "I'm just not good at showing emotions."

He taught me that real love doesn't drain you, it fills you. Real love doesn't leave you questioning your worth; it affirms it daily.

He reminded me that choosing myself was not selfish, it was necessary. It was survival. It was the first step toward reclaiming my peace.

Still Writing Our Story: Finding Real Love

Finding real love didn't happen overnight for me, it unfolded slowly, steadily, and with intention. That real love is Steven.

As our relationship grew, so did our shared experiences. What began with weekend visits gradually expanded into long vacations, cruises, and time intentionally carved out just to enjoy one another. We laughed easily. We explored new places. We created memories that felt light, joyful, and free. Something I hadn't realized I had been missing for so long.

We genuinely had fun together, the kind of fun that doesn't require effort or performance, just presence. Steven wasn't into sports when we first met, but over time I opened his eyes to something I've always loved: basketball. I introduced Steven to my favorite team, the Boston Celtics, and what started as casual interest quickly became a tradition. Every basketball season, we travel to Boston to see a game. It's something we look forward to together, a ritual filled with excitement, anticipation, and shared joy.

Somewhere along the way, Steven found his own favorite player. Watching Steven cheer, react, and talk about the game with genuine enthusiasm still makes me smile. It reminds me how real love expands you, how it invites you into new worlds simply because you care about the person standing beside you.

One night, we attended a Brooklyn Nets game. During a break, Steven was chosen from the crowd to go down onto the court for a chance to win a prize. At first, he was reluctant, uncomfortable being in the spotlight. But with encouragement from me, and a kind woman nearby who reminded him it was a once-in-a-lifetime experience, he agreed to go.

Steven didn't win the big prize that night, but when he returned to his seat holding the prize he did receive, the excitement on his face was priceless. His smile was wide and genuine, full of joy. In that moment, I realized how special it is to witness someone allowing themselves to fully experience happiness.

In many ways, Steven and I opened each other's eyes to life. He reminded me to slow down, to enjoy moments without overthinking, to laugh without guarding my heart so tightly. I reminded Steven to step outside his comfort zone, to try new experiences, and to embrace joy without hesitation.

We didn't try to change each other, we complemented each other. That balance, the shared curiosity, and the mutual encouragement taught me that love isn't about fixing or saving someone. It's about walking alongside one another, choosing peace, and building something rooted in respect, joy, and truth.

We are still writing our love story, one moment at a time. It hasn't been fast or flashy. It has been a slow burn, growing quietly over more than a decade, rooted in trust, patience, and mutual respect. What I have now with Steven is steady, certain, and real.

There is no rush, no pressure to arrive at some perfect ending, just two people choosing each other, growing together, and allowing the future to unfold naturally. We are drifting forward hand in hand, carrying the lessons of the past without being bound by them.

Pain shaped me, but it no longer defines me. Love now feels safe, grounded, and honest. As we look toward the future, I do so with confidence and peace, knowing that marriage is not a distant dream, but something in the very near future.

Our story is still being written, and for the first time, I am not afraid of what comes next.

I am excited.

Closing Reflection: From Pain to Power

For years, I believed pain was my identity.

Now I know pain was only my teacher.

It taught me what I would never accept again. It taught me that healing is not weakness; it's courage. It taught me that I could carry the weight of my world and still rise.

When I look back now, I don't see the woman who was broken. I see the woman who rebuilt herself from the pieces.

I see the mother who stayed strong for her son. The survivor who finally said, "No more." The woman who chose herself when everyone else had chosen to overlook her.

The pain I carried became my strength.

Call to Action: Choose Yourself Today

To every reader holding this book, hear me clearly: **you do not have to stay where pain lives.**

Choose yourself. Choose peace over chaos. Choose healing over hiding. Choose boldness over silence.

Take a moment to reflect:

1. Where are you still carrying pain that no longer belongs to you?

2. What boundaries do you need to set to protect your peace?

3. How can you choose yourself today, even in one small way?

4. What kind of love are you accepting: the kind that breaks you or the kind that builds you?

Write your answers. Speak to them aloud. Live them daily.

Because you are worthy. You are beautiful. You are enough.

The pain you carried is not the end of your story; it's the beginning of your boldness.

Reflective Journal: From Hurt to Healing

1. What pain from your past are you still carrying, and how is it affecting you today?

2. What does "choose yourself" look like in your current season of life?

3. Who or what have you had to let go of to find peace?

4. Write a letter to your younger self beginning with: "You survived more than you realize, and now it's time to..."

5. Describe what healthy, peaceful love looks like to you, whether it's from yourself or someone else.

Final Affirmation: *Say this with your hand on your heart: Even when I was hurting, I kept moving. Even when I was silent, I was surviving. And now, I am thriving.*

CHAPTER 5

RISING THROUGH THE FIRE: A MOTHER'S STRENGTH, A WORKER'S JOURNEY

Affirmation: *Even when the world doubted me, I kept believing. Even when my vision failed me, my faith gave me sight.*

Opening: Rising Through Fire

Fire can burn, destroy, and reduce things to ashes. But fire can also refine, strengthen, and purify. My life has contained both kinds of fire.

There were seasons when the flames threatened to consume me through betrayal, exhaustion, heartbreak, loneliness. Moments when I thought I couldn't take another step, couldn't endure another blow, couldn't survive another disappointment.

There were also seasons when that same fire refined me, shaping me into a woman of resilience, courage, and unshakable faith. When the heat that should have destroyed me instead burned away everything false, everything weak, everything temporary, leaving only what was essential and true.

This chapter is about that fire: the one that burned away fear and revealed my strength. It's about rising through the challenges of motherhood and work, about holding on to faith when sight failed, and about surviving a world that often underestimated me.

At the center of it all was my son, David; my reason to keep going when I wanted to stop. My purpose when everything else felt purposeless. His small hands, his laughter, his very existence reminded me that quitting was not an option.

He didn't ask to be born into struggle; but his presence transformed my struggle into strength.

David's Birth Into a House of Abuse

David came into this world on January 19, 1989. Not into peace or joy, but into conflict and control.

His cries filled a house heavy with tension. The air was thick with unspoken resentment, with arguments that simmered just beneath the surface, with a coldness that no baby's warmth could thaw.

As I held him, his tiny body wrapped in a blue blanket, his eyes squeezed shut against the bright lights, I whispered a promise through tears: "You will not live the life I lived. You will know love."

But I was whispering that promise in a house where love felt conditional, where affection was rationed, where my requests for help were met with indifference or anger.

When David cried in the middle of the night, I handled it alone. When he needed to be fed, changed, soothed, I did it all while his father slept undisturbed in the next room.

I begged for help. Just a little help. Just someone to hold him for ten minutes so I could take a shower, eat something, close my eyes without fear of missing his cries.

His father's cold response was always the same: "That's your job, not mine."

So I did it all. Working full-time at the police department. Waking every two hours to feed a hungry baby. Changing diapers. Doing laundry. Grocery shopping with David; I had no one to watch him.

I went to sleep exhausted, with David in my arms, tears soaking the pillow, whispering prayers into the darkness: "God, please give me strength. I can't do this alone. But I will if I have to."

David's birth didn't happen in a house full of love. But it gave birth to something else in me: determination.

He became my reason to rise. My reason to believe that life could be different. My reason to fight when I wanted to surrender.

The balancing act: Work, College, and Motherhood

When people say "doing it all," they often imagine balance: work, family, personal time, all flowing smoothly together in perfect harmony.

My "doing it all" was pure survival. There was no balance. There was only motion, constant motion, because stopping meant everything would fall apart.

At the Town of Greenvale Police Department, I worked full-time. No matter how tired, sick, or worn down I was, I showed up.

Rent didn't care about my exhaustion. Bills didn't wait for healing. Daycare didn't offer grace for a single mother barely holding it together.

I showed up early. I stayed late when needed. I did my job with excellence because I had a little boy depending on me, and failure was not an option.

The teasing didn't stop just because I became a mother. The whispers continued about my glasses, about jealousy, about being "just a secretary" who would never be more.

But they didn't stop me. I had David waiting for me at home, and he needed me to succeed.

Even with everything on my shoulders, I enrolled in college.

I wanted David to see that education mattered. That even when life got hard, even when you were tired beyond words, you kept learning, kept growing, kept reaching.

I studied late into the night with David beside me, his little hands gripping crayons while I highlighted textbooks. He colored pictures while I typed papers, the sound of the keys filling the room like a steady reminder that we were building something together.

I rocked him to sleep with one arm while holding a book in the other, whispering vocabulary words into his hair like lullabies.

I was exhausted beyond measure, but I was determined beyond exhaustion.

Motherhood was my greatest blessing and my hardest test.

David's father offered no help, no partnership, no relief. When I asked for a small break, just an hour to breathe or gather myself, the answer was always the same: "That's your job."

So, I carried the weight alone.

There were mornings when I woke up after two hours of sleep and still went to work with a smile. Not because I wasn't breaking, but because I refused to let the struggle break me.

Somewhere in the fire, I learned that strength doesn't mean you don't feel pain. It means you move forward anyway.

My faith became quieter but deeper. Most days it wasn't shouted; it was whispered. Sometimes it was nothing more than, "Lord, help me make it through today."

And He did.

The fire didn't destroy me. It refined me.

Closing Reflection

Looking back now, I see that those years were not meant to end me. They were shaping me. Preparing me. Teaching me how to survive with grace and rise with faith.

I may not have worn a uniform, but I showed up every day in the fight. I may not have had perfect vision, but faith gave me sight.

And through it all, I kept going.

Call to Action

If you are walking through your own fire, don't give up. Acknowledge what you're facing. Hold onto whatever anchors you. Keep showing up even when no one notices. Your consistency is building something greater than you can see.

Reflective Journal

Take a moment to reflect:

What fire in your life has tested you the most?

How has that fire changed or strengthened you?

Who is your reason to keep going?

What has faith taught you about yourself?

Final Affirmation: *Even when the fire was intense, I did not quit. Even when I was exhausted, I showed up. Even when I felt alone, I was never abandoned. I was refined, not destroyed. And I am still rising.*

CHAPTER 6

FINDING MY VOICE IN AFRICA

Affirmation: *I thought I was traveling to another continent, but I was really traveling back to myself.*

Monday, July 24, 2023: The Day Everything Changed

That Monday morning, July 24, 2023, began like any other: coffee brewing, traffic humming outside my window, the familiar rhythm of another workweek beginning.

Until it didn't.

The phone rang at 9:47 a.m. I glanced at the screen and saw the hospital's number. My stomach dropped before I even answered.

"Jennifer, you need to get here. Your brother isn't going to make it."

I grabbed my keys, my hands shaking, my heart pounding with hope and dread tangled together like twisted rope. I rushed out the door, my mind racing through traffic lights and turn signals, praying I'd make it in time. Praying for a miracle. Praying that maybe, just maybe, they were wrong.

But before I could even reach the hospital, another call came through.

This time, the words stopped me cold: "His heart wasn't strong. He passed away."

I pulled over, gripping the steering wheel until my knuckles turned white, tears blurring my vision. Part of me didn't believe it. Part of me didn't want to.

Bruce was more than a brother. He was a piece of my childhood, a link to memories both good and bad. The one who teased me, made me laugh, and sometimes made me cry. He wasn't perfect (none of us were), but he was my blood. My family. My history.

For years, I had wished he would protect me, stand up for me, love me the way I needed. I had hoped for reconciliation, for healing, for one more conversation where we could finally say the things we'd left unsaid.

That chance was now gone.

The complicated mix of grief and resentment crashed over me all at once: sorrow for his death, and sorrow for everything he never was. Pain for losing him, and pain for never truly having him.

I cried until I couldn't anymore. Then, in the stillness that followed, sitting in my car on the side of the road with emergency lights blinking, I made a quiet promise to myself:

Something has to change.

Wednesday, July 26: Flying Into the Unknown

Two days after losing Bruce, I boarded a plane bound for Johannesburg, South Africa.

My heart was still raw, my eyes still swollen from tears. Part of me wanted to cancel the trip, to stay home and grieve in familiar surroundings, to attend the funeral and say goodbye properly.

But something deeper told me not to. Somewhere in my spirit, I felt that maybe this was divine timing. The journey I was about to take would help me make peace with everything I'd been carrying, not just about Bruce, but about my whole life.

When the plane lifted into the clouds, I closed my eyes and whispered a prayer: "God, if this is where my healing begins, help me not to run from it."

For sixteen hours, I floated between two worlds: the one I was leaving behind (grief, loss, unfinished conversations) and the one waiting to transform me (a continent I'd never seen, a soil my ancestors once walked, a healing I didn't yet understand).

Grieving Across Oceans

The first days in Johannesburg passed in a blur of jet lag and sorrow.

While the group explored the city, marveling at its energy and diversity, I slipped away to make funeral arrangements from thousands of miles away. Time zones blurred. My days became nights. My grief had no schedule.

I spent nights on WhatsApp calls and email chains, trying to coordinate services I couldn't attend. I approved the obituary, discussed casket options, spoke with family members still reeling back home. Planning a funeral from across the world felt like a strange act of love: present but absent, involved but distant, grieving while pretending to be okay.

I didn't write my brother's obituary, my cousin did. I found myself reading it while sitting in the heart of Africa, the land our ancestors once called home. Bruce and I didn't have the kind of brother-sister bond that made every memory easy to hold, yet there I was, thinking through his life, imagining the paragraphs I might have written. The irony wasn't lost on me.

I cried quietly in hotel bathrooms. I cried on tour buses. I cried in the shower where the water could hide my tears.

Grief meets you wherever you are. And sometimes, that's exactly where healing begins.

Zimbabwe: The Forgiveness Exercise—Angel Walk

Early one morning, before we went on safari, we completed an exercise about forgiveness. The question that haunted me was simple but profound: *How do you forgive someone who has hurt you your entire life?*

It was deep, raw work. I gave voice to the hateful email I had received and finally named the years of abuse I had endured from my brother Calvin. The emotional weight of it all had left me utterly exhausted.

After a brief discussion, we began the Angel Walk exercise. One by one, we stepped into the center of the path, where the host of the retreat held you in an endearing hug and whispered empowering words. Words that can only be described as a sacred undoing. The kind of words that quietly dismantle every lie you have ever believed, every hurt you have ever carried, and replace them with an unshakeable truth and a peace that wraps tenderly around every broken place.

Then, as you walked through the line of people on either side, like a bride moving down the aisle to meet her groom, there was no fanfare, only whispered words of encouragement, like gentle wings lifting you forward one step at a time.

When it was my turn, my heart beat like thunder in my chest. The old weight of fear and shame pressed against me, the teasing, the judgment, the long shadow of Calvin's years of cruelty. Behind me, I felt the small girl I had once been, the one from seventh grade, watching with wide, quiet eyes, wondering if she would finally be set free.

But the walk was nothing like I had feared. The whispers surrounding me were soft, tender, and full of hope, like a warm breeze slowly lifting the heaviness from my shoulders. Tears streamed freely, not from sorrow alone, but from a strange and soaring relief. As if a chain I had carried so long, and had forgotten its weight had finally, mercifully, broken.

In that luminous, fragile moment, I understood that forgiveness was not a gift I was giving Calvin. It was a gift I was finally giving myself. It meant reclaiming my voice, my peace, and my power. I could let him go, not because what he did was acceptable, but because I refused to carry it one step further.

That morning marked the first true step of my journey to true healing and back to myself.

Victoria Falls: Baptism in the Mist

The next day, we went to Victoria Falls, located on the border between Zimbabwe and Zambia in southern Africa. The sheer scale of the falls was breathtaking. A wall of water thundering into the gorge below, sending mist high into the sky, rainbows glinting in the sunlight.

Amid the roar and spray, there was a strange, peaceful beauty. I closed my eyes and whispered into the sound, letting the falls carry my words: *"Bruce, I love you. I forgive you. And I forgive myself."*

The water thundered on, relentless and eternal, and in that rhythm, I felt something inside me shift. The anger, the grief, the long-held pain, they seemed smaller somehow; softened by the vastness of this place. Here, in the heart of Africa, on the land our ancestors once called home, I could release what I had carried for so long.

And in that release, I found peace.

Closing Reflection: When Healing Has a Passport

Healing doesn't always happen in hospitals or therapy rooms. Sometimes it happens on a plane, in a forgiveness circle, or on a patch of red soil beneath your bare feet.

Being in Africa taught me that healing can be holy even when it's messy. It taught me that forgiveness isn't weakness; it's reclaiming power. It taught me that grief can live beside gratitude, and that it's possible to mourn what you've lost and still celebrate who you're becoming.

I went to Africa with a broken heart and returned with a renewed spirit.

Bruce's death closed one chapter, but the Motherland opened another.

That journey didn't just change me. It awakened me.

Call to Action: Find Your Own Healing Ground

Maybe you can't fly across the ocean right now. Maybe your "Africa" is a quiet park bench, a church pew, a beach at sunrise, or a walk around your block after a long day.

Wherever it is, go there with intention.

Take off your shoes if you can. Feel the ground beneath you. Breathe deeply and allow yourself to be present. Let that space become sacred, even if only for a few minutes.

Speak forgiveness out loud, even if your voice trembles. Release the names that still weigh heavy on your heart. Forgiveness does not mean forgetting or excusing harm; it means choosing peace over captivity.

Allow yourself to grieve what you've lost; relationships, years, dreams, versions of yourself that never got to exist. In the same breath, give yourself permission to celebrate who you are becoming.

Write a new promise to yourself in that space. Keep it sacred. Revisit it when old wounds resurface.

Your healing does not have to look like mine. It does not require a passport or a plane ticket, but it does require courage.

Take the first step. Your healing ground is waiting.

Reflective Journal: Returning to Yourself

Take a quiet moment and write honestly, without judgment or rushing.

1. What grief are you still carrying that you have not fully allowed yourself to release? Where do you feel it in your body?

2. Who is someone you need to forgive, not because they deserve it, but because you deserve peace?

3. What is your personal "healing ground"? Describe the place where you feel most connected to yourself and to peace.

4. Write about one person, situation, or season you need to let go of with love rather than bitterness. What would releasing it change for you?

5. Imagine your next chapter. How will you honor your healing and protect your peace as you move forward?

Write until your heart feels lighter. This is not about perfection, it is about returning home to yourself.

Final Affirmation

Say this with your hand on your heart:

Even across oceans, I found myself again. Even through grief, I chose healing. Even through loss, I reclaimed my voice. I release what no longer serves me.

I honor where I've been and who I am becoming. I am free to move forward in peace.

CHAPTER 7

FROM QUIET STEPS
TO BOLD STAGES

Opening Affirmation

Even when fear tried to hold me back, I stepped forward anyway. Each step became proof that boldness was already living inside me.

Learning to Live Carefully

For most of my life, I learned how to move carefully.

Not carefully in the sense of thoughtfulness or intention, but carefully out of fear. Fear of being seen. Fear of being judged; afraid of becoming a target again. I learned how to navigate rooms by reading the temperature of other people's moods. I learned when to speak and when silence would keep me safer. I learned how to make myself smaller so others could feel more comfortable.

I stepped carefully around other people's opinions.

Carefully around family expectations.

Carefully around pain that felt like it might spill over if I moved too fast.

Careful became my survival language.

In my family, in relationships, and eventually in my workplace, I mastered the art of quiet endurance. I showed up. I did what was expected. I smiled when I was hurting. I swallowed words that deserved to be spoken. I convinced myself that if I stayed agreeable, helpful, and invisible, life would hurt less.

But careful living has a cost. It keeps you alive, but it also keeps you trapped.

I didn't realize how much of myself I had hidden until I began to feel the weight of carrying everything alone. The exhaustion wasn't just physical; it was emotional. It was spiritual. It was the tiredness that comes from pretending you're okay when you're barely holding yourself together.

I wasn't living boldly.

I was surviving quietly.

The Habit of Shrinking

Shrinking didn't start in adulthood. It started when I was young, when laughter followed me through hallways, when nicknames stuck harder than kindness, when my glasses became a reason to mock instead of a tool to see.

Back then, shrinking felt like protection.

If I didn't raise my hand, they wouldn't notice me.

If I didn't speak, they couldn't laugh.

If I stayed quiet, maybe I'd make it through the day without being hurt.

That habit followed me into adulthood.

I shrank in conversations where my voice mattered. I stayed silent in rooms where I had earned the right to speak. I accepted behavior I shouldn't have tolerated because I didn't want to be labeled difficult, emotional, or ungrateful.

Silence became familiar. Familiar felt safe.

But silence has a way of turning inward. What you don't say out loud doesn't disappear, it settles inside you. It shows up as anxiety, self-doubt or the quiet belief that maybe you really are too much or not enough.

For a long time, I didn't even realize I was shrinking. I just thought this was who I was.

When Whispers Turned Into Questions

The shift didn't happen all at once.

It started with whispers, quiet questions that interrupted my routine:

Why do I feel invisible in my own life?

Why does keeping the peace cost me so much?

What would happen if I stopped apologizing for existing?

At first, I ignored those questions. They felt dangerous. Asking them meant I might have to change something, and change felt terrifying.

But the whispers grew louder.

They followed me into sleepless nights.

They sat beside me during long drives.

They lingered after conversations that left me drained instead of fulfilled.

Eventually, those whispers turned into prayers.

Not bold prayers. Not confident ones. Just honest ones.

"God, I'm tired."

"God, I don't know how much longer I can keep doing this."

"God, I need help, even if I don't know what that help looks like."

Those prayers didn't come with immediate answers, but they cracked something open inside me.

For the first time, I allowed myself to admit that surviving wasn't enough anymore. I wanted to live.

The first step people often think transformation begins with is a dramatic moment, a declaration, a breakthrough, a bold announcement.

Mine didn't.

Mine began with a single realization: life doesn't change until you move.

Not a leap.

Not running.

Just move.

One step.

One step toward honesty.

One step toward healing.

One step away from silence.

That first step was internal. It was deciding that my feelings mattered, even if no one else validated them yet. It was acknowledging that the pain I had endured; bullying, loss, workplace dismissal, emotional wounds, was real and deserved attention.

I stopped telling myself to "just be strong" and started allowing myself to be honest.

That step felt small, but it shifted everything.

Once you take one step, standing still no longer feels like safety, it feels like stagnation.

Fear's Favorite Timing

Fear is strategic.

It doesn't show up when you're already broken down, it waits until you start to rise. Until you consider doing something different. Until you think about choosing yourself.

Fear doesn't knock politely. It barges in with questions meant to paralyze you:

What if you fail?

What if they laugh again?

What if you tell your truth and people judge you for staying too long, for enduring too much, for not leaving sooner?

What if you discover you're not as strong as you hoped?

Fear showed up loudest when I thought about using my voice.

My whole life, I had been taught, directly and indirectly, to keep things inside. Family matters stayed in the family. Pain was private. Strength meant silence.

The idea of speaking openly about bullying, grief, abuse, and resilience felt like peeling back scars that had barely healed. It felt vulnerable. Exposed. Dangerous.

But I had learned something crucial through years of quiet endurance:

Every time I stayed silent, fear won.

Every time I chose boldness, I reclaimed a piece of myself.

I was tired of handing my power to fear.

Boldness Begins Quietly

Boldness didn't announce itself with confidence.

It arrived gently, in moments that looked ordinary from the outside but felt monumental on the inside.

It showed up when I said no without explaining myself.

When I stopped overextending just to be liked.

When I refused to feel guilty for resting.

It showed up when I set boundaries with people who were used to unlimited access to my time, my energy, and my emotional labor.

It showed up when I said, calmly but firmly, "I won't accept being spoken to that way anymore."

That sentence terrified me the first time I said it. My heart raced. My hands shook. I waited for backlash.

Something unexpected happened instead.

I felt lighter.

Boldness, I learned, doesn't always feel brave in the moment. Sometimes it feels uncomfortable. Sometimes it feels lonely. Sometimes it feels like you're doing the wrong thing simply because it's unfamiliar. But discomfort is not the same as danger and growth often disguises itself as uneasiness. One of the most pivotal steps I took was logging into my first therapy session.

I remember staring at the screen before clicking "join," wondering if I should cancel. Wondering if my pain was "bad enough" to justify help. Wondering if I could really say everything out loud.

But I joined anyway. And for the first time, I said the words I had swallowed for years: "I'm not okay." "I'm tired of being strong." "I need help."

There is something powerful about hearing your own truth spoken aloud. Once it leaves your mouth, it no longer has permission to haunt you in silence.

That moment didn't fix everything, but it began something honest. And honesty, I learned, is the foundation of boldness. Each small step rewired how I understood courage. Courage wasn't loud. It wasn't fearless. It wasn't dramatic. Courage was movement. It was being afraid and moving anyway. It was choosing yourself even when it would have been easier to disappear. It was letting go of who you had to be to survive so you could become who you were meant to be. I wasn't bold yet, not fully. But I was no longer shrinking. And that was the beginning.

Boldness in the Workplace: Standing Tall at Greenvale

For many years, the workplace felt like a continuation of the hallways I thought I had left behind.

At the Greenvale Police Department, I worked hard, showed up consistently, and carried myself with professionalism. Yet beneath the surface, I felt the familiar sting of whispers, side glances, and assumptions. The teasing that once followed me in school had simply changed uniforms and vocabulary. Comments about my glasses. Questions about my competence. Subtle dismissals disguised as jokes. At first, I handled it the way I always had: quietly.

I cried in private. I replayed conversations in my head, wondering what I could have said differently. I questioned myself instead of questioning behavior that never should have existed in the first place. But something inside me had already begun to shift.

As I grew bolder internally, I realized I could no longer allow other people's opinions to define my worth. I had spent decades proving myself through consistency, integrity, and dedication. I was done shrinking to make others comfortable.

Boldness at work didn't come with confrontation or raised voices. It came with presence. I lifted my head. I straightened my posture. I walked into rooms knowing I belonged there.

Instead of shrinking when gossip surfaced, I chose dignity. Instead of defending myself to every rumor, I let my character speak. Instead of internalizing negativity, I anchored myself in truth.

There were days it still hurt. Days when isolation felt heavy. Days when walking away seemed easier than staying.

But every day I chose dignity over bitterness; I reclaimed another piece of myself.

I learned that boldness in the workplace isn't about proving people wrong. It's about knowing who you are, even when others refuse to see it.

Faith at My Desk

One of my quietest yet boldest acts was bringing my faith into my workday.

For years, I prayed silently, almost apologetically, as if my faith needed to stay hidden. But as I stopped shrinking in other areas of my life, I stopped hiding this part of myself too.

I kept a small devotional book in my desk drawer. I read it during breaks. I whispered affirmations before difficult meetings. I prayed openly, softly, but unapologetically, when days felt heavy.

Instead of letting the environment shape my spirit, I allowed my spirit to shape how I showed up.

Faith wasn't something I turned on and off anymore. It became a steady presence, reminding me that I wasn't alone, even when I felt isolated.

Slowly, the workplace stopped feeling like a battlefield and began to feel like a place where my resilience could stand tall.

Boldness as a mother: Teaching by Example

Boldness also transformed the way I showed up as a mother.

David had seen me at my lowest, exhausted, overwhelmed, stretched thin. He had seen the nights I stayed up late studying, the mornings I showed up to work with a smile after crying the night before. He watched me juggle responsibilities while carrying wounds no one else could see. But he also watched me rise. He saw me choose myself. He saw me speak up. He saw me keep going when quitting would have been easier.

Boldness as a mother wasn't about having all the answers. It was about showing him what resilience looks like in real time.

I wanted him to know that life can be unfair and still be meaningful. Stumbling doesn't mean failing and falling doesn't disqualify you from getting back up. I wanted him to learn courage by watching me live it. Through every challenge, I hoped he would see this truth: even when life feels heavy, you can still move forward, one bold step at a time. I didn't want him to inherit bitterness. I wanted him to inherit courage. And I believe he did.

From Whispered Prayers to Bold Faith

My faith journey changed alongside my sense of self. For years, my prayers were whispers spoken in the dark:

"God, if You're there, help me."

"God, I don't know how much more I can take."

"God, just get me through today."

Those prayers were honest, but they were cautious, like I was afraid to ask for too much.

As I stepped into boldness, my prayers changed too.

They became declarations.

I spoke affirmations out loud, even when they felt unfamiliar. I read scripture with intention, declaring it over my life instead of just reading it quietly. I refused to let fear or shame silence my conversations with God. Faith stopped being passive and became active.

I trusted that every step I took was ordered, even when I couldn't see the full path. I believed that my pain had purpose, even when I didn't yet understand it. I leaned into the truth that weakness wasn't something to hide, it was where grace showed up most powerfully. Each prayer became an act of courage.

The Invitation That Changed Everything

Then came the phone call.

It was a phone call, the kind that made my hands tremble and my heart race. An invitation to speak at **TEDx Clarkstown, New York**, scheduled for May 2025. I remember holding the phone, replaying the words in my mind to make sure I had heard them correctly. *You've been selected to speak.*

Me? The girl who learned to survive by staying quiet. The woman who spent decades hiding behind silence.

That call wasn't just an opportunity, it was confirmation. Confirmation that my voice mattered, that my story mattered, and that everything I had survived had purpose.

Preparing to Be Seen

Preparing for TEDx wasn't just about writing a speech. It was about facing myself.

Each draft forced me to revisit pain I had buried; bullying, grief, workplace dismissal, emotional wounds that still ached when touched. There were nights I sat alone, staring at my screen, tears blurring the words.

Am I ready to tell the world?

Am I strong enough to say this out loud?

The answer was never a confident yes.

It was always a trembling maybe.

But I had learned something essential: boldness doesn't wait for confidence. It moves in spite of fear. I practiced in front of mirrors. Sometimes my voice cracked. Sometimes I had to stop, breathe, and remind myself why I was doing this.

Not for applause, not for validation: for the people still hiding behind silence. And for the woman I was becoming.

The Day My Knees Trembled—and I Stood Anyway

May 2025 arrived faster than I was ready for. Backstage at TEDx Clarkstown, my knees shook. My heart pounded so loudly I could hear it in my ears. Old lies crept in, whispering doubts I thought I had outgrown.

But I remembered my affirmation: *Even when my knees tremble, I can stand. Even when my voice shakes, I can speak.* I closed my eyes and whispered one last prayer: "God, let my story help someone." Then I walked onto the stage anyway.

Finding My Voice on the Red Circle

As the lights warmed my face and the room grew quiet, something inside me shifted. I began not with my name, but with a question that lived deep in my spirit: "Has anyone here ever been bullied?" Hands lifted. Heads nodded. The room connected instantly.

I spoke about the global cost of bullying, how it follows people from childhood into adulthood, into workplaces, into their sense of self. I spoke about shame, silence, and survival.

I spoke about rising. As the words flowed, fear loosened its grip. My voice grew stronger. My message felt bigger than just my story. The girl who once hid had become the woman who spoke. I thought about the younger version of myself, sitting in the back of classrooms, praying not to be noticed. I thought about the years of swallowed words and silent endurance, the fear of being judged that followed me into every room. This moment wasn't just for me, it was for every version of myself who once believed she didn't matter.

When the Applause Faded

When I finished speaking, the room rose to its feet.

Applause filled the space, and for a moment everything felt unreal. The lights, the faces, the sound washing over me like a wave. Tears filled my eyes, not from pride, but from release. The girl who once tried to disappear had just stood in the brightest light and spoken her truth. But when the applause faded and I stepped off the red circle, something unexpected happened.

I felt quiet. Not empty, just still.

Boldness doesn't end on the stage. The real work begins when the spotlight turns off and you return to everyday life, carrying both the weight and the wonder of what you've just done.

David: My Son, My Greatest Witness

David found me first.

When he hugged me, years of struggle collapsed into that single moment. He had seen me cry in private and rise in public. He had watched me work through exhaustion, study late into the night, and keep going when quitting would have been easier.

He looked at me and said, "Mom, I'm proud of you." Those words meant more than any standing ovation ever could.

My boldness had become his inheritance, not because of what I said on stage, but because of how I lived every day. He learned resilience by watching me endure. He learned courage by watching me choose myself.

In that moment, I understood something deeply: legacy isn't built in grand gestures. It's built in consistency, honesty, and courage lived out loud.

Family Shifts: Being Seen Differently

My family relationships have always been layered and complex.

Growing up, teasing, misunderstanding, and emotional distance shaped many of our dynamics. I was often seen as the quiet one, the one who endured without complaint.

After TEDx, something shifted.

They saw me not just as Crystal, the one who survived, but as a woman who had risen, a woman whose voice mattered beyond our family walls.

Some reached out with pride. Others with curiosity. A few with silence.

I learned something important: boldness doesn't require universal approval. It requires self-respect.

When you stop shrinking, people either adjust, or step back.

Either way, you keep moving forward.

Friends, Colleagues, and the Power of "Me Too"

Messages began arriving in the days and weeks that followed.

"You spoke for me." "I've never told anyone this before, but I was bullied too." "I thought I was alone until I heard you."

Even at the Greenvale Police Department, where I once felt dismissed or misunderstood, colleagues approached me differently.

"You said what I've been afraid to say."

"Thank you for being brave."

My story gave others permission to acknowledge their own.

That's when I realized: boldness is contagious.

When one person tells the truth, it opens space for others to do the same.

Hope Without a Roadmap

After TEDx, I expected doors to swing open immediately. They didn't. There was no instant flood of invitations or overnight momentum. Instead, there was something quieter, hope. I hope that the moment mattered. I hope that my story will travel farther than my fear ever had; hope that purpose doesn't always arrive with fireworks, it unfolds step by step. TEDx awakened a belief deep inside me: my voice could reach places my pain once kept me from.

Jamaica: When My Story Became a Mirror

One of the first doors that opened led me to the University of the West Indies in Montego Bay, Jamaica.

Standing before students, faculty, and community members, I saw reflections of my own journey, young people navigating bullying, adults carrying childhood wounds, survivors learning how to name their pain.

After my talk, a young woman approached me with tears in her eyes. "I thought I was the only one who felt this way," she said. At that moment, I knew my story was no longer just mine. It had become a mirror, reflecting possibility back to those who had forgotten it.

Coming Full Circle: Youth and Community

In July 2025, I spoke with young people involved in a community youth program connected to the Greenvale Police Department.

These were young people I had quietly supported for years. But now I stood before them not just as Jennifer Taylor, but as someone who had turned pain into purpose.

One young man raised his hand and asked, "Do you think someone like me could ever be like you?" I smiled and answered honestly, "You already are. Boldness starts the moment you believe you matter." His eyes lit up. That moment reminded me why I speak.

September 2025: Boldness Expands

That fall, I was invited to speak to the parents of a girls' empowerment organization dedicated to mentoring young girls into confident, self-aware young women.

The room was filled with parents who wanted better for their daughters, parents determined to protect them from wounds they themselves still carried.

As I spoke, I realized my message wasn't just for the girls. It was for the adults guiding them. Healing a generation begins by equipping the ones who raise them.

An Event in Washington, D.C.

Later that month, I was invited to participate in a national author and speaker event in Washington, D.C.

Sitting on that panel, surrounded by leaders, creatives, and advocates, I felt grounded, not intimidated, not hesitant.

So grounded that the moderator commented on my confidence and presence. During my remarks, I addressed the nickname that once humiliated me: Grandma Dynamite.

Instead of rejecting it, I reclaimed it. "Yes, I'm Grandma Dynamite," I said, "and now I plan on blowing up the world with my story." Laughter filled the room. Applause followed. What once tried to diminish me had become fuel.

October: A Summit and a Reminder

October—Anti-Bullying Month, didn't unfold the way I expected. School opportunities didn't materialize. Disappointment lingered briefly.

Then another door opened. I was invited to speak at a leadership and personal development summit, sharing my story with an audience committed to growth, healing, and transformation.

After my talk, the organizer sent me a video message. In it, her young daughter spoke about how inspired she felt, how my words made her believe she could be brave too.

I cried. Sometimes one inspired child is more powerful than a room full of applause.

How the Stage Became My Healing

People assume speakers are healed before they step on stage. The truth is, my healing happened on the stage. Each time I spoke, another layer of pain lifted. Every word spoken out loud lost its power to hurt me in silence. The stage didn't make me bold. It revealed the boldness that had been growing all along.

Faith That Carried Me

I never stood alone. Backstage, trembling, I whispered, "God, be with me." And he was. "My grace is sufficient for you, for my power is made perfect in weakness." My trembling wasn't my weakness. It was strength revealed.

When Purpose Becomes Clear

Looking back now, I can see it clearly; every step mattered. The careful steps. The fearful steps. The bold ones I almost didn't take.

At the time, none of it felt strategic. It felt messy. Emotional. Uncertain. But purpose rarely announces itself fully formed. It reveals itself gradually, through obedience, courage, and a willingness to keep moving even when the path is unclear.

I didn't wake up one day knowing I would stand on stage or speak about bullying, resilience, and healing. I simply knew I couldn't stay silent anymore.

That decision, to stop shrinking, changed everything. Purpose didn't come from being fearless. It came from being faithful to the next step.

Boldness Isn't a Destination

For a long time, I believed boldness was something you arrived at. A finish line you crossed once you finally felt confident enough.

I was wrong. Boldness is practice. It's choosing to speak even when your voice shakes. It's honoring boundaries even when guilt creeps in. It's continuing forward even when progress feels slow or invisible. Some days, boldness looks like standing on a stage. Other days, it looks like getting out of bed and choosing yourself again.

Both matter. Both count. And both require courage.

What I Know Now

I know now that silence protects nothing, it only delays healing. I know now that the parts of my story I once tried to hide are the very parts that connect me to others. I know now that fear doesn't disappear when you're bold, it just loses its authority. And I know now that my voice was never the problem. I was never "too much." I was never "not enough." I was becoming.

The Legacy I'm Leaving

When I think about the life I'm building and the legacy I'm leaving, I don't measure it by applause or invitations.

I measure it by this:

Did I live honestly? Did I stop shrinking? Did I choose courage when fear tried to silence me? If my story teaches anything, I hope it teaches this:

You don't have to be fearless to be bold. You just have to be willing.

Call to Action: Take Your Next Bold Step

This is your moment to pause and reflect. What bold step have you been avoiding? Is it telling the truth to yourself or to someone else? Is it setting a boundary you've been afraid to enforce? Is it asking for help instead of carrying everything alone? Is it sharing your story, even if only with one trusted person? Is it choosing healing instead of silence?

Write it down.

Name it.

Then take one step toward it.

Not tomorrow.

Not when you feel ready.

Today.

Because boldness doesn't happen all at once.

It grows step by step, choice by choice.

Every time you choose courage over fear, you rewrite your story.

Journal Reflection: Stepping Fully into Yourself

Take time with these questions. Write freely and honestly.

1. Where in your life have you been shrinking to feel safe?

2. What fear has been holding you back, and what truth can replace it?

3. What is one bold step you've already taken that you're proud of?

4. How would your life change if you stopped minimizing your voice?

5. What does walking in boldness look like for you right now?

There are no wrong answers, only honest ones.

Final Affirmation

Say this slowly. Say it out loud. Let it settle. *Even when my knees trembled, I stood. Even when my voice shook, I spoke. Even when fear whispered "hide," I chose to shine. My boldness became my breakthrough. And I am still becoming.*

CHAPTER 8

FROM BULLIED TO BOLD

Affirmation: *Even when the world tried to silence me, I found my voice. Even when I was bullied into hiding, I became bold enough to shine.*

Opening: The Transformation

If someone had told the little girl with thick glasses, the one teased as "Grandma Dynamite"—that one day she would stand on a stage and share her story with the world, she would have laughed in disbelief.

She would have said, "Not me. I'm too broken. I'm too invisible. I'm too afraid."

But here I am. From the porch in Mount Vernon where I once sat alone in my graduation gown, to the office where coworkers whispered behind my back, to the bathroom stalls where I cried in silence; every moment of my journey carried me here.

To this voice. To this purpose. To this boldness.

This chapter isn't just about what I endured. It's about what I became.

From bullied to bold. That is my story. And if it's mine, it can be yours too.

Looking Back at the Girl with Glasses

When I close my eyes, I can still see her, the little girl sitting in the back of the classroom, trying to hide behind glasses that magnified her eyes until they became the joke of the day.

She never asked for attention, yet it always found her. Not for her kindness. Not for her intelligence. But for what made her different. "Grandma Dynamite." "Four eyes." "Ugly."

Each word was a pebble thrown at a fragile window, and every day she wondered when she would finally shatter.

That girl learned early how to build walls. How to smile when laughter stung. How to say "I'm fine" while breaking inside. How to cry only in the dark, where no one could see.

I didn't know then that the very things that made me stand out would one day make me strong. Those glasses, once my shame, became part of my testimony. That voice, once silenced, became my strength. The laughter that once broke me became the fuel that built me.

The Power of Therapy

For years, I carried my story like a locked box, afraid of what would spill out if I opened it. The bullying. The abuse. The grief of losing both parents too soon. The loneliness of being overlooked and underestimated. Silence didn't protect me. It suffocated me. I didn't realize how desperate I was for air until I stepped into therapy.

Logging into that first Zoom session, my palms were sweating, my heart racing.

What if I don't belong here? What if they think I'm weak? What if I say it out loud and nothing changes? But once I started speaking, something broke open, not destructively, but liberatingly. Like a dam finally releasing what it had held for too long. I cried about my father's last words. About missing my mother's voice. About years of hiding pain behind practiced smiles.

My therapist didn't judge me. She listened. She held space. She reminded me that telling the truth isn't weakness, it's courage. Therapy didn't erase my pain. It gave me language for it. And with language came power.

Daily Affirmations: Rewriting the Script

For years, my mind replayed insults like a broken record:

"You're not enough." "You're ugly." "You'll never be more than this."

Bullying doesn't end when the teasing stops. It lingers in the mind, shaping how you see yourself long after the voices are gone.

So, I decided: I would rewrite the script.

At first, affirmations felt awkward. Forced.

"I am beautiful." "I am strong." "I am enough." My reflection didn't believe me at first. But I kept speaking anyway.

Day after day, the words planted roots. Affirmations didn't erase my past. They healed my present. Paired with prayer and scripture, they became my armor:

"I am fearful and wonderfully made."

"No weapon formed against me shall prosper."

"God is within her; she will not fall."

Eventually, the truth grew louder than the lies.

Living Boldly Every Day

Boldness didn't end with TEDx. It became how I live. Boldness in the morning begins with affirmations before the world speaks first. Boldness at work means showing up with dignity at the Greenvale Police Department and letting my integrity speak louder than whispers. Boldness in family means boundaries without guilt. Boldness in faith means trusting God even when the path isn't clear. Boldness is not loud. It is consistent.

From Victim to Victory

I once carried the label of victim. But healing taught me this truth: I was never powerless. I was becoming powerful. Victory isn't the absence of pain. It's the decision to rise anyway.

A Global Mission: The Cost of Bullying

As I began speaking, I realized my story wasn't unique, it was universal. Bullying follows people into adulthood, into workplaces, into mental health struggles. Studies show it contributes to anxiety, depression, absenteeism, lost productivity, and long-term health effects. The cost isn't just financial, it's personal. Behind every statistic is a silent voice. That's why my mission is bigger than just my own voice. I speak for the child mocked for being different. For the adult belittled in silence. For anyone still carrying invisible scars.

Final Reflection & Call to Action: From Silence to Boldness

Boldness didn't save my life all at once.

It saved it choice by choice. Choosing truth over silence. Choosing healing over hiding. Choosing faith over fear.

Call to Action

1. Speak one truth out loud.

2. Write one affirmation.

3. Take one bold step.

4. Believe you are enough.

You don't have to stay silent. You were never meant to.

Journal Reflection

1. What does bold look like for you right now?

2. What lies need to be replaced with truth?

3. Write three affirmations for who you're becoming.

4. What step can you take this week?

5. What would your younger self need to hear?

Final Affirmation

I am not my pain. I am my purpose. I am no longer bullied. I am bold. My voice matters. My story matters. I matter. And I will never be silent again.

CHAPTER 9

A BOLD LEGACY

Affirmation: *I am not my pain. I am my purpose. My story is my legacy.*

Looking Back: From Silence to Boldness

If you had told the little girl with thick glasses sitting in the corner of the classroom while classmates mocked her, that one day she would be called bold, she would have shaken her head in disbelief.

If you had told the teenager who cried herself to sleep after losing her mother that she would one day write a book to encourage others, she would have whispered, "Not me."

If you had told the young woman hiding bruises behind long sleeves that she would one day stand on a TEDx stage, speaking her truth while strangers wiped tears from their eyes, she would have laughed bitterly and thought: *They don't know my life.*

But here I am. I was bullied. I was silenced. I was abandoned. I was bruised. I overcame it. Yet, I did not stay there. God brought me through every valley: not just so I could survive, but so I could live; not just so I could heal, but so I could help others heal; not just so I could carry a story, but so I could leave a legacy.

This is what it means to go from bullied to bold.

It means transforming pain into purpose. It means letting your scars become your story. It means refusing to let the worst moments of your life have the final word.

David: My Living Legacy

Of all the people my story has touched, none matter more to me than my son, David.

David didn't ask to be born into struggle. He didn't ask to grow up in a home where survival sometimes spoke louder than comfort, where love existed but life still felt heavy at times. But even then, God had a plan.

From the moment I held him in my arms on that cold January morning in 1989, I whispered promises into his tiny ears: that he would know love, that he would be protected, that his story would not have to mirror my pain.

He saw me fight battles that most children never see. Coming home from long shifts at the police department, pushing through exhaustion, showing up even when I wanted to collapse. He saw me cry, but he also saw me rise.

That is what I passed down: not my bruises, but my boldness; not my silence, but my survival.

David became the first male grandchild in our family to graduate high school. As he crossed that stage, my tears were not like the lonely tears I once carried, they were tears of victory.

David tried college, stumbled, and came home. I told him, "Coming home isn't failure. It's preparation." He kept pushing forward, one season at a time.

Eventually, he found steady work caring for the elderly. That job shaped him in ways I couldn't have predicted. It taught him that compassion is strength, that patience is power, and that service matters, whether anyone applauds it or not.

There was a time he dreamed of building a future in a different direction, and he worked hard toward it. Life didn't unfold exactly the way he expected, but it never diminished his determination or his heart.

When I look at David, I see resilience. I see perseverance. I see proof that cycles can be broken.

He is not defined by one moment or one outcome. He is defined by his character, and by the way he continues to move forward. David is my living legacy.

For Survivors Everywhere

David may be my living legacy, but this story is for every survivor still fighting to believe they are more than their pain. For the woman who cries herself to sleep behind a mask of strength. For the teenager who dreads the walk to school because of what waits in the hallways. For the worker silently praying for one peaceful day without whispers or mockery. For the man carrying grief he cannot name and shame he doesn't know how to release. For the child who feels invisible in their own home and wonders if anyone sees them. This legacy is not just mine. It is ours.

Survivors carry silent power. Every scar is evidence of a battle endured. Every tear shed in secret is proof that you felt deeply and still chose to keep going.

You may not feel bold today, but boldness lives in you already. It showed up every time you got back up. Every time you whispered, "I can't" and did it anyway. Every time you survived another day when giving up felt easier.

That's boldness, and it's already yours.

Your Voice Matters

Silence may have once protected you, but it cannot heal you. Your voice is your power. It doesn't have to be loud to matter. It just must be yours.

Speak to a friend who will truly listen. Tell your therapist what you've been carrying alone. Write in your journal the words you're afraid to say out loud. Whisper to God the prayers you've kept locked inside.

But speak.

Because your truth is the first step to freedom. Your story may be the key that unlocks someone else's healing.

Your voice, the one you've kept quiet for so long, is part of the legacy you were always meant to leave.

A Shared Legacy

The legacy I leave is not about being special. It's about being willing.

I am willing to heal, even when it hurts. I am willing to speak, even when my voice shakes. Willing to transform pain into purpose, even when staying silent felt safer.

If every survivor told their story, imagine the chains that would break. Imagine the boldness that would rise. Imagine the children who would grow up knowing they're not alone. Imagine the adults who would finally exhale and say, "Me too. I survived that too." That's the legacy I want not just for me or for David, but for all of us.

A legacy of broken silence. A legacy of shared strength. A legacy of boldness that spreads like wildfire, lighting the way for those still walking in darkness.

Boldness in Schools, Workplaces & Communities

Legacy isn't built on isolation. It's built in a community, in the places where we live, work, learn, and grow.

In Schools - Boldness means teachers seeing the quiet child in the back of the classroom and asking if they're okay.

It means parents asking their kids how they feel, not just what they scored on their test.

It means students choosing kindness over cruelty, standing up for the kid being bullied instead of looking away.

In Workplaces - Boldness means ending toxic cultures that normalize gossip, mockery, and disrespect.

It means leaders protecting people as fiercely as they protect profits.

It means coworkers speaking up when they see someone being mistreated instead of staying silent to keep the peace.

In Communities - Boldness means refusing to look away when someone is struggling.

It means checking on neighbors, offering safe spaces, breaking generational secrets that keep families trapped.

It means turning faith into action and love into service.

Change begins with us; in our classrooms, our offices, our homes, and our hearts.

The Power of Boldness

Boldness has been the common thread through every chapter of my life. It was there when I stood up after being knocked down. It was there when

I spoke after years of silence. It was there when I chose myself for the first time, even when it felt selfish, even when it felt scary.

Boldness is not the absence of fear. It is the decision to move forward anyway. It is faith in action. It is hope with hands. It is light in dark places. It is what turns pain into purpose, and purpose into legacy.

It transforms victims into victors, survivors into storytellers, and the broken into the bold.

Call to Action: Live Your Bold Legacy

You have walked this journey with me, through pain, through growth, into boldness.

Now, it's your turn to walk boldly forward.

Your legacy begins now. Not tomorrow. Not when you're ready. Not when you've healed completely or fixed all your flaws.

Now.

Here's how:

1. Speak life daily. Use your voice to uplift yourself and others. Say the affirmations. Speak the truth. Share the story.

2. Model boldness. Let people see you rise, stumble, and rise again. That is courage in real life.

3. Protect your peace. Set boundaries that honor your worth. Say no when you need to. Walk away when staying would cost you your spirit.

4. Serve others. Mentor someone still finding their way. Be the voice for those still searching for theirs.

5. Plant seeds of hope. Every truthful word you speak is a seed. You never know whose life will change because you chose not to stay silent.

Legacy is not built in tomorrow. It is built in today's choices. Speak. Heal. Shine. That's how you live your bold legacy.

Journal Reflection

Take a quiet moment to write freely and honestly:

1. What does legacy mean to me personally?

2. What values do I want to leave behind for my family or community?

3. What stories or truths am I still afraid to share, and why?

4. How can I use my story to inspire someone else?

5. What does living "boldly forward" look like in my daily life?

Close your eyes, take a deep breath, and write this affirmation in your own handwriting:

"I am not my pain. I am my purpose. My story is my legacy."

The Mirror I See Now

For so long, I looked into mirrors that lied to me; mirrors that told me I was too much or not enough. Mirrors that reflected ridicule instead of resilience. Mirrors that showed brokenness instead of beauty.

But now, when I look in the mirror, I see something different.

I see a woman who survived what should have destroyed her.

I see a mother who raised a son with love even when she didn't always receive it herself.

I see a survivor who became a storyteller.

I see scars that become stories.

I see pain that became purpose.

I see boldness.

And I know that the little girl with the thick glasses, the one they called Grandma Dynamite—would be proud of the woman standing in her place.

Closing Truth

Legacy is not about perfection. It's about perseverance. It's not about never falling. It's about rising every time you do. It's not about erasing the past. It's about transforming it into fuel for the future.

My legacy is this: I refused to stay bullied; I chose to become bold. I refused to stay silent; I chose to speak. I refused to let pain have the final word; I chose purpose instead. Now that legacy is yours too. Because when one of us rises, we all rise. When you choose boldness, you don't just heal yourself, you ignite healing in others.

This is my legacy.

And now, it is yours too.

FROM BULLIED TO BOLD — A NEW BEGINNING

Affirmation: *Even when the world tried to bury me in silence, I rose. I am no longer the bullied girl. I am the bold woman.*

The Journey Comes Full Circle

As I write these final words, I see the road behind me; long, winding, and filled with valleys I never thought I'd climb out of.

I see the little girl hiding behind glasses too thick for her small face, trying to disappear into the back of the classroom.

I see the teenager sitting on the porch in her graduation gown, waiting for a celebration that never came.

I see the young woman covering bruises, whispering prayers in secret, wondering if life would ever feel different.

I see the mother rocking her baby boy in the dark, promising him a better life while tears soaked her pillow.

I see the woman in therapy finally speaking her truth after decades of silence.

And I see the woman standing on the TEDx stage, voice trembling but growing stronger with each word, declaring: "I am not what was done to me. I am bold."

This is not the end of my story. It is a new beginning.

A beginning where I no longer carry shame. A beginning where my voice is louder than my fear. A beginning where my purpose is clearer than my pain.

That beginning is available to you too.

Looking Back Without Shame

For years, I carried my past like a heavy bag of bricks, convinced that my story disqualified me from ever being more than what I'd endured.

I thought the bullying meant I was fundamentally flawed. I thought the abuse meant I was unlovable. I thought the silence meant my voice didn't matter.

But shame is a liar.

What once made me hide now makes me powerful. The thick glasses that defined "Grandma Dynamite" are now part of my testimony. The teasing that tried to break me became the foundation of my resilience. The grief that should have destroyed me became the soil where faith grew deeper roots. The bruises I hid behind long sleeves became proof that I survived what was meant to kill my spirit. None of it broke me. All of it built me.

Every insult became a seed of strength. Every betrayal became a lesson in boundaries. Every loss became a reminder of life's fragility, and the importance of living fully while we can.

Now, when I look back, I don't see shame. I see survival. I see strength. I see boldness born in silence and strengthened through faith.

I see a woman who refused to stay buried.

The Woman I Became

The woman I am today no longer hides behind fear. She stands tall, speaks truth, and leads with love.

She is the mother who raised her son in strength and faith, teaching him that resilience is inherited not through perfection, but through perseverance.

She is the professional who turned gossip into grit, who lets her work speak louder than whispers, who chose dignity over defensiveness.

She is the speaker who turned pain into purpose, who stepped onto stage with trembling knees and a steady mission, sharing her story so others wouldn't feel alone.

She is the believer who knows every valley prepared her for victory, every closed door redirected her, and every "no" protected her from the wrong "yes."

I am no longer the survivor hiding in silence.

I am a storyteller who speaks boldly.

I am the truth-teller refusing to shrink.

I am the bold woman who will not return to the shadows.

And the best part? I am still becoming.

Still growing. Still healing. Still rising.

The Legacy I Leave Behind

Legacy isn't measured in money, titles, or applause. It's measured in impact.

My son David is living proof that cycles can be broken. He didn't inherit my pain, he inherited my persistence. He didn't learn victimhood; he learned resilience. He grew up knowing that struggle doesn't define you; how you rise from struggle does.

But my legacy stretches beyond my family. It belongs to every child who has ever been bullied and thought they were the problem. It belongs to every adult still carrying childhood wounds they've never spoken about. It belongs to every survivor reading these words and whispering, "If she could rise, so can I." This book is part of my legacy.

Every speech I've given. Every affirmation I've spoken. Every tear turned into testimony. Every moment I chose boldness instead of silence.

That is my legacy. Boldness multiplies when it is shared. When one person finds their voice, it gives others permission to find theirs. When one survivor speaks, others realize they don't have to carry their story alone. My legacy is not about me. It's about us.

Final Charge: Live Boldly Forward

Your story is not over. It's only the beginning.

You were not created to live small or silent. You were not designed to shrink or hide. You were not meant to carry shame that was never yours to hold.

You were born to rise. So today, right now, make a choice:

Break the cycles that broke you. Don't pass down the pain, pass down the perseverance.

Speak the truth that once silenced you. Use your voice to tell the story only you can tell.

Live the legacy you want future generations to inherit. Be the ancestor your descendants will be proud of.

Choose boldness over bitterness. Let your scars become stories that heal others.

When one of us rises, we all rise. When you choose boldness, you don't just heal yourself, you ignite healing in others. You become living proof that transformation is possible.

This is my legacy. And now, it is yours too.

A Love Letter to My Younger Self

Before I close these pages, I want to speak to the girl I used to be, the one who felt unseen, unheard, and unworthy.

Dear Crystal,

I see you. Sitting in the back of the classroom, shoulders hunched, hoping no one notices the thick glasses or the way your heart races when laughter starts behind you. I see the tears you cry quietly into your pillow at night, the pain you swallow because you don't believe anyone would understand, or worse, care. You learned early how to survive in silence, how to make yourself small just to get through the day.

I want you to know this: you were never invisible. You mattered then, even when it didn't feel that way. Every tear, every moment you endured, every word you held back was shaping a strength you couldn't see yet. The voice you were afraid to use was never weak, it was just waiting for the right time to rise.

Now I write to you as the woman you are becoming. I carry your memories with me, but I no longer carry your shame. I've learned that the laughter didn't define me, and the names didn't tell the truth about who I was. I still get scared sometimes. I still feel that old ache now and then. But I showed up anyway. I stand taller. I choose myself. I honor you by refusing to disappear.

And this is your future, Crystal: you survive, and then you rise. You become a woman who breaks cycles instead of repeating them. You become a mother who leads with love, strength, and protection. You become a voice for the little girls who sit in the back of the room praying not to be seen. One day, you will stand on stages and speak of the very pain they tried to bury you with. You go from bullied to bold. From overlooked to fully seen. From quiet survival to fearless presence. From hidden pain to visible strength.

I am so proud of you, not for being perfect, not for never falling, but for getting back up every single time. For choosing courage when it would have been easier to give up. For believing, even on the hardest days, that there was more waiting for you.

Keep going, baby girl. Your past did not break you. Your present is proof of your strength. And your future is brighter than you can imagine.

With all my love,
The woman you became

To Every Reader Holding This Book

If you've made it to this final page, I want you to know something:

You didn't pick up this book by accident. Maybe you saw yourself in my story. Maybe you're still carrying wounds from childhood. Maybe you're hiding behind a smile while breaking inside. Maybe you're wondering if boldness is even possible for someone like you. It is. You don't have to have it all figured out. You don't have to be fearless. You don't have to be perfect. You just have to be willing. I am willing to take one step. I am willing to tell you the truth. I am willing to try one more time. That's all boldness requires. If I can go from "Grandma Dynamite" to a TEDx stage, from silence to purpose, from bullied to bold, so can you.

The Invitation

This is not goodbye. This is an invitation. An invitation to join the movement of survivors becoming storytellers. An invitation to trade shame for strength, silence for speaking, and fear for faith. An invitation to go from bullied to bold. Will you accept it? Will you pick up the mirror that tells the truth and finally see yourself as you really are; strong, resilient, worthy, and bold? Will you tell the story you've been carrying in silence? I believe you will. You've already proven you're a survivor. Now it's time to prove you're a thriver.

Welcome to the Rest of Your Life

Your journey is not over. Your boldness is just beginning. From this moment forward, you walk differently. You speak differently. You live differently. Because you are no longer bullied, you are bold. And the world will never be the same because you will find your voice.

Final Words

Thank you for walking this journey with me. Thank you for reading my story, for holding space for my pain, for celebrating my boldness.

But more than that, thank you for seeing yourself in these pages. For recognizing that your story matters too. For choosing to rise.

This is my story. But it's also yours. We are the silenced who find our voices. The bullied who became bold. The broken who chose to heal. Together, we are unstoppable. So go now. Live boldly. Speak truthfully. Love fiercely. Rise repeatedly. The world is waiting for your voice.

Affirmation: The Final Declaration

Say this one last time, with everything in you: *Even when the world tried to bury me in silence, I rose. I am no longer a bullied girl. I am a bold woman. My voice matters. My story matters. I   matter. And I will never, ever be silent again. From this day forward, I walk in boldness. This is my declaration. This is my legacy. This is my life. From bullied to bold, forever.*

THE END... AND THE BEGINNING